STRANGE FROM HASTINGS

A CORNUCOPIA OF BIZARRE DEATHS & UNSOLVED MURDERS

VOLUME ONE

By the same author

Strange Exits from Hastings Volume Two

Notable Sussex Women: 580 Biographical Sketches

Jack the Ripper at Last? The Life and Crimes of George Chapman

Railwaywomen: Exploitation, Betrayal and Triumph in the Workplace

Women of Victorian Sussex: Their Lives, Occupations and Dealings with the Law

Mary Raleigh Richardson: The Suffragette Arsonist who Slashed the Rokeby Venus

Published 2020
This imprint 2023
ISBN 9781904109365
Printed in England by Mixam

The Hastings Press
hastings.press@gmail.com
www.hastingspress.co.uk

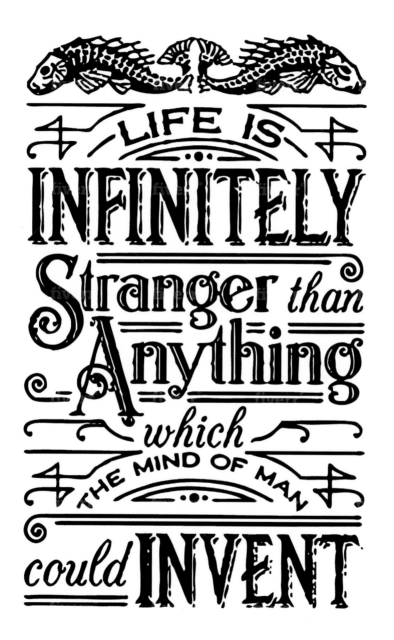

LIFE IS INFINITELY Stranger than Anything which THE MIND OF MAN could INVENT

INTRODUCTION

Whilst consulting newspaper archives for a different local history project, time and again a report of a bizarre death, an unsolved murder or an inexplicable suicide caught my eye. I became drawn into the stories, and sometimes found myself trying to solve a murder or explain a baffling death. Eventually I gave in to the stories' repeated bids for my attention, and took time out to research and publish them as an unusual addition to the social history of our towns.

This book represents a tiny fraction of the many lives cut short by suicide, accident or homicide in the Hastings area between 1800 and 1950. This selection has been carefully chosen to include only unsolved, baffling or bizarre unnatural 'exits'. In some chapters, readers are invited to join me in turning 'amateur detective' to try to solve mysteries left unresolved when the cases were closed. I have included snippets of local history related to the stories, plus a few lengthy 'digressions' about some interesting local characters.

EXPLANATORY NOTE

Our local paper, the *Hastings & St Leonards Observer*, is abbreviated to *HSLO* throughout. As a rule of thumb, an inch is about 2.5cm, a foot is 30cm, a yard is just under a metre, and a pound in weight is roughly half a kilo. The currency throughout the book is £ s d — pounds, shillings (s) and pence (d). There were twelve pence (12d) in a shilling (1s) and twenty shillings in a pound.

ACKNOWLEDGEMENTS & SOURCES

I am grateful to my dear friends Stephanie Hedger and David Green for their time and expertise in assisting me with genealogical sleuthing and proof reading.

The sources used were the British Newspaper Archive, newspapers.com, Gale Historical Newspapers, *The Times* Historical Archive, Ancestry, FindMyPast, FamilySearch and eBay. For photos and facts I thank Miranda Pender and Mollie Tucker (re: Joseph James), Raymond Gunn (re: Joe Titchener), and the owners of numerous websites, including www.chesshistory.com, guestling.org. uk, leweshistory.org.uk, 1066Online.com and www.arthurlloyd.co.uk, Richard Pollard, Steve Peak and the late Ion Castro. Thank you to all my readers for making this the fastest-selling Hastings local history book of all time.

Helena Wojtczak BSc (Hons) FRHistS
hastings.press@gmail.com

CONTENTS

1804 Capricorn's Revenge	7
1830 Baronet's Folly	9
1845 Life and Sole	11
1848 The Cook of Caterina Villa	13
1848•1849 The Family Poisoner	27
1849 Chair Trigger	39
1870 Three Men Down	43
1877 Lethal Liniment	47
1881 (Un)natural Death	53
1889 The Killer Spoke	57
1891 Train Track Tragedy	59
Interlude: The Hospitals Opposite Hastings Pier	71
1892•1900•1904 The Curse of the Bones	73
1897•1900 Mrs Bertel's Misfortunes	81
1893 Fatal Friendship	85
1896 Look Before You Leap	91
1899 The Mystery of the Missing Gun	95
1900 The Final Crossing	101
1904 For the Want of a Pocket	105
1905 High Wire Horror	107
1910 The Infirmary Enigma	113
1911 One Revolver; Two Dead	117
1920 Murder on the Hastings Express	133
1927 Corpse-in-the-Wood	139
1928 Dying For a Pee	145
1929 Freak Wave In a Heatwave	147
1930 Born To Be Wild	151
1932 Indian Clubbing	155
1932 Don't Try This at Home	169
1935 Mystery Walk	171
1935 Riddle of the Range	173
1939 The Piermaster's Secret	177
1948 Cliff Edge Conundrum	183

An officer of the 40th Foot Regiment.

1804

CAPRICORN'S REVENGE

HALTON

Between 1798 and 1823 the Mount Road end of Priory Road was the site of army barracks. In 1797 the government bought from former mayor Edward Milward (senior) thirty acres known as Gallows Field, a tract of land 'beautifully situated on an elevated spot' at Halton. The first barracks built were small and were abandoned after two years. Prompted by renewed threats of a French invasion, they were rebuilt in 1804 with more extensive accommodation which could house a greater number of troops, cavalry, infantry and artillery.

Within weeks of the first soldiers moving in someone was killed. This occurrence, one may think, is not altogether surprising, given that there were a lot of young, strong, fit, competitive men, trained to fight and kill, and weapons were easily available, and yet the culprit was not of the human species.

The tragedy occurred on Monday 1st October and the report appeared in *The Times* the following Friday. It read:

> The Major of the 40th [Foot] Regiment has a large goat, vicious in nature, with whom the soldiers were in the habit of playing. A fine young man, servant of the Colonel, was teasing the animal for a considerable time, and was advised by many of his comrades to desist, but he would not; at length, the enraged animal got the unfortunate young man against a wall, and gored him so dreadfully, that he died on being taken to the hospital. The animal's horn penetrated above the left knee, ran up the thigh, and dividing the scrotum passed into the abdomen, and tore out the bowels.

Sadly, all that was recorded about the unfortunate lad was his age: he was just eighteen.

The barracks fell into disuse and were auctioned in 1823. The land was used for houses, shops and pubs for the labouring classes. A century later the area was again redeveloped, providing modern housing and open green spaces.

Sir Frederick Francis Baker, Bt. (1772–1830)
Engraver James Heath, after John Hoppner.

Fairlight Mill.

1830

BARONET'S FOLLY

FAIRLIGHT

Sir Frederick Francis Baker, Bt, was the son of Sir George Baker, senior physician to 'mad' George III. Frederick was a brainy fellow, gaining his BA and MA at Oxford by age twenty-four. He dedicated his young life to cultural pursuits, becoming a fellow of both the Society of Antiquaries and of the Royal Society of Arts.

When he reached middle age, Sir Frederick married an MP's daughter, after which his luck turned bad: his London house was razed to the ground by a fire that swept through it in 1824. Soon after being rebuilt, it was nearly destroyed again by a blaze in the house next door in 1827.

It is said that these things 'always come in threes'.

In late September 1830 Sir Frederick, his wife and their four children, aged between four and fourteen, visited Hastings for the winter, staying in a guest house in Wellington Square. On 1st October they 'took an airing in a fly' to Fairlight Down, stopping at a picturesque windmill, built in 1819 and owned by Edward Milward. Sir Frederick ascended the stage to teach his children the mechanisms by which a windmill operates.

> The miller, unconscious that any person occupied the stage at the time, put the sweeps in motion, one of which struck Sir Frederick on the head with great violence; an alarm was immediately given, and the most scientific surgical aid promptly had recourse to.

Carrying him into the fly, the baronet's horrified family told the driver to hurry to Pelham Crescent, where Mr Benjamin Travers was staying with his sister, Mrs Gooch. A senior surgeon at St Thomas's Hospital, and future surgeon-in-ordinary to Prince Albert, Travers performed an operation, but, alas, days later, Sir Frederick died without regaining consciousness.

The coroner's inquest concluded that death was accidental, and was caused by Sir Frederick being so short-sighted that he did not notice a gigantic piece of timber swirling towards his head. He was buried in St Mary's Chapel (now called St Mary-in-the-Castle) on 15th October. The press noted that many tradespeople of Hastings attended the funeral to mourn the tragic loss of a wealthy customer.

Bad luck continued to plague the baronet's family after his death: both of his sons were admitted to a private lunatic asylum in 1846, where they were confined for the remainder of their lives.

The mill burned down in 1869 and North's Seat occupies the site.

The Old Ship at Pett Level.

A sole.

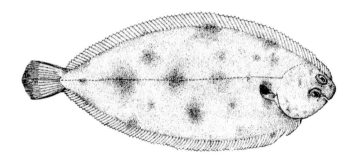

1845

LIFE AND SOLE

CLIFF END BEACH

Joseph Simmons, John Hyde, Walter Adams and George Mann were four tough and brawny fishermen of Hastings. On the evening of Monday 16th June they enjoyed a very successful catch off the coast of Pett. At about 9.30pm they landed their boat at Cliff End to visit the Ship Inn, a convivial hostelry built on the beach about a hundred years earlier.[1]

Having consumed five jugs of beer they returned to the boat. As Joe and George were hauling in a net, George impulsively snatched up a small live fish, grinned and said gleefully: 'I will show you how to eat a sole!' Throwing his head back he popped it into his mouth, but it jumped out. He tried a second and a third time, then shouted, 'You little beggar, won't you go down?' Although the fish struggled and wriggled, he managed to get it a little way into his throat, where it promptly became stuck. He attempted to pull it out, but it would not budge. Joe opened his knife and tried to spear it by the tail and drag it out, to no avail. Next, he fetched a length of thin rope and put a loop into George's throat to lasso the obstinate creature. As he tugged on the rope George's head suddenly dropped and he became motionless.

It was midnight, and some of the Preventive Service men were present, on the lookout for smugglers. One of them dashed off to get medical help. The nearest doctor, John Innes Pocock, lived a mile away at Winchelsea and by the time he reached the scene an hour had passed and George was dead.[2]

At the conclusion of an inquest held at the Ship Inn before Coroner Nathaniel Polhill Kell, the jury returned a verdict of 'Accidental death by attempting in a joke to swallow a small fish.'

George Mann, who was thirty-eight, left six dependent children, the youngest only three years old. His widow, Sarah, supported them by setting herself up in business as a fishmonger, employing her son James as an assistant. Two of George's sons followed his lead and became fishermen.

References: *Brighton Gazette* 26th June 1845. George Mann's death received wide coverage in the national press, including the *Illustrated London News* and some Scottish newspapers.

---

1. The Ship Inn existed until 1931, when it was destroyed by a storm.
2. We shall hear more of Mr Pocock in 'The Family Poisoner'.

A watercolour from the early 1840s. West Hill Road, looking east. The Assembly Rooms and St Leonards Hotel (now the Royal Victoria) can be seen in the centre right. The figures in the foreground are standing near the site of the forthcoming Caterina Villa.

Caterina Villa for sale. It was purchased by Miss Moore.

CATERINA VILLA,

A delightful Marine Residence, at St. Leonards, Hastings.

MR. LEIFCHILD has received instructions from the Proprietor to SUBMIT to PUBLIC AUCTION, at Garraway's, on Wednesday, November 24, at Twelve for One, in One Lot, the above most desirable FAMILY VILLA, which possesses great advantages, in a healthy and elevated situation, from which it commands magnificent sea views. Caterina Villa has been erected within the last two years in the most substantial and perfect manner; the elevation is strictly Tudor, and is greatly admired, and the interior is designed with every attention to comfort and convenience. It contains large entrance hall and staircase, handsome dining and drawing rooms and library, china closet and store room, five capital bed-rooms well fitted with closets, landing and water closet; the basement, which is light and dry, includes kitchen and scullery, housekeeper's room, pantry, good wine and beer cellars, poultry yard and houses, and other useful domestic offices. The stabling, which is conveniently placed, consists of a double coach-house, two-stall stable, harness room, lofts, and two servants' bed-rooms. This very desirable villa is delightfully placed on a well-kept lawn, which is tastefully planted and surrounded by thriving plantations and pleasure-grounds, and there is a most excellent kitchen garden well stocked.

1848

THE COOK OF CATERINA VILLA

WEST HILL ROAD

In 1848 Caterina Villa was one of only three houses on West Hill Road. It was situated at the summit of the hill, adjacent to the archery ground. Built in 1846 in Tudor style, it boasted several elegant reception rooms, five bedrooms and a commodious basement containing a large kitchen and other service rooms. Behind the house was a stable and a coachhouse with rooms above for servants. The grounds were encircled by a stone wall, with a pair of carriage gates on the south side. These were kept locked, with a bell supplied for visitors.

Mary Ann Catherine Moore, a wealthy, middle aged spinster, bought the villa to share with her brother John, a newly-retired army surgeon. The cook, Mary Ann Newman, known as Ann, had worked for Miss Moore for twenty-seven years. Three recently-engaged servants — coachman Henry Mitchell, footman James Grey and housemaid Jane Cannon — completed the household.

On Sunday 12th November the Moores left the villa at 10.35am and were driven in their carriage to the Baptist chapel at Wellington Square. The cook closed and locked the gates behind them and busied herself preparing lunch. After dropping off the Moores and the footman at the chapel, the coachman stabled the horse and carriage in the Castle Mews and walked back to join his colleague in one of the gratis pews.

The housemaid waited for the carriage to depart, then straightened Miss Moore's bedroom, leaving the window open an inch. She descended to the kitchen to find the cook, a short, stout woman, seated on a chair, one stocking removed, changing a bandage on her leg. After a brief chat the housemaid left at 11.10am to attend the service at nearby St Leonard's chapel.

When the Moores arrived home at 12.45pm the footman, Grey, rang the gate bell repeatedly, but the cook did not appear. He climbed over the wall, unlocked the gate and went down the steps to the kitchen. He tried the door, which Ann always kept unlocked, but found it was locked. Peering through the window he saw no sign of her. The carriage trundled up to the front door but nobody had a key, so Dr Moore and Grey circled the house searching for another way in. The stable doors, closed when they left, were wide open, and so was the sash window of Miss Moore's ground floor bedroom.

Grey climbed in and saw the room had been ransacked. A dressing case, a chest of drawers, a jewel case and a trunk had been forced open. Dr Moore checked his own room; a portmanteau had been disturbed but nothing was missing. Grey descended the internal stairs to the basement in search of the cook. At the foot of the stairs an old garden spade stood upright, propped against a hamper. Its blade, worn thin and sharp by heavy use, was bent out of shape and covered in blood.

Grey then discovered the cook, Ann Newman, lying on her back in a bend of the passage. He called out to Dr Moore and stared at the sickening scene. There was so much blood: Ann's head lay in a puddle of it and more bespattered the walls and even the ceiling. By some miracle, she was still breathing, so Dr Moore sent for their physician, Robert Cumming of 29 Marina.

Ann's injuries were ghastly. She had sustained a deep cut on the left of her skull and six more on the right and her right ear was completely severed. Two wounds were so deep they sliced open the skull and 'laid bare the brain, part of which oozed out'. Some of the main branches of her temporal artery had been severed, which is why blood had spurted out.

Even Dr Moore, an ex-army surgeon, was 'much agitated' by the sight. He ordered the servants not to tell his sister; he would break it to her himself, gently and with a glass of brandy and some smelling salts close at hand.

In those days there were no paramedics or casualty departments, so once her wounds were dressed Ann was put to bed in the vain hope that she would recover. By some miracle she lingered for two days, until, at 8.50am on Tuesday 14th November, she succumbed, becoming the first murder victim in the new town of St Leonards.

An inquest was held at the Assembly Rooms the next day. Coroner John Goldsworthy Shorter[1] and a jury of nineteen men walked up the hill to Caterina Villa to view the scene and the victim. Ann's head 'presented a frightful spectacle', especially the 'hideous chasm down to the brain'. Glad for a walk in the cold, fresh air the jury returned to the rooms, where they heard depositions from the Moores and their servants. The verdict needed no deliberation: it was clearly a case of 'wilful Murder against some person or persons unknown'.

Miss Moore was deeply affected by the senseless slaughter of her most loyal servant. She offered a reward of £50, to which the Secretary of State added £50 from public funds. Posters and handbills were printed and exhibited across town: anyone supplying information that led to the conviction of the murderer would receive part or all of the reward and given immunity from prosecution.

At 4pm on 15th November, Ann Newman was interred in the small burial ground at the side of the Wesleyan Methodist chapel in Norman Road.

Constable Number 16, Henry Sheather, aged thirty-eight, had been a policeman for eight years, prior to which he worked as a watcher and gamekeeper for the militia that predated the police.[2] He relished the challenge of applying his twenty years' experience of tracking footprints to the detection and capture of a killer.

1. J.G. Shorter (1804–1857) town clerk and coroner, committed suicide by shooting himself in the head. His own deputy conducted the inquest.
2. Sheather (1810–1882) was the uncle of Thomas Sheather, who appears in 'Train Track Tragedy'.

Having examined the scene, Sheather concluded that the assailant, armed with a chisel, had concealed himself in the archery grounds. He must have waited until the cook was alone, climbed the dwarf wall by the chicken-shed and entered the stable, 'to procure some instrument' to break 'whatever locks might defy the application of a chisel'. He crossed to the villa, descended the area steps and entered the basement. Through the open door of the knife room he spotted several garden tools and grabbed a spade. At this point he was confronted by the cook. He used the spade to strike her on the head, knocking her down, then stood over her and inflicted several more ferocious blows, 'with such violence', opined Sheather, 'that had they fallen on the neck, they must have severed the head from the body'.

The killer left the bloodied spade at the foot of the stairs and locked the kitchen door. Climbing the stairs to the ground floor he made a brief foray into Dr Moore's room then moved on to Miss Moore's, helped himself to her most valuable jewellery, lifted the window sash wide, climbed out and retraced his steps to the archery ground.

Henry 'Turf' Hyland was arrested because in 1845 he had desecrated a grave in order to steal jewellery. But Turf had an alibi and besides, Sheather was convinced that the intruder was someone intimately acquainted with the household: he knew when to strike and where the small valuables were kept, and the ferocity of the attack pointed to a personal grudge against the cook.

Sheather discovered that the previous coachman, John Pearson, had been dismissed two weeks previously for 'irregular habits' and 'neglect of duty'. He had often quarrelled with Ann and vowed vengeance against her. That night Inspector John Campbell[1] tracked down Pearson at the Hastings Arms in George Street, arrested him and marched him to Hastings Gaol.

Pearson was twenty-three. His father, Francis, was from Battle, but had worked in Ireland in the 1820s, where he married and started a family. In 1833, when John was eight, the Pearsons moved to St Leonards. Francis became the toll collector at Hollington turnpike gate, and when John was fourteen he saw his father viciously bludgeoned over the head by robbers. Later Francis became a fly driver[2] and the family moved into Wellington Mews in Hastings.

In his teens John was a waiter at the Royal Oak in Castle Street. His aunt was the landlady, having married the licensee, William Yates. In early 1848 John became a fly driver for Thomas Skinner at Harold Mews, behind the Horse and Groom in Mercatoria. He left after a week to become coachman to Miss Moore, but nine months later, on 31st October, she dismissed him for bad conduct.[3]

1. One of the first twelve constables sworn into the Hastings police on its inauguration in 1836.
2. A fly is a horse-drawn cab for public hire. Later, Francis became a self-employed bath-chair man, wheeling elderly or infirm visitors around town and along the seafront. After his death in 1851, his wife Letitia took over his business, employing another teenage son to push the chair.
3. Thomas Skinner's fly company continued for over a century, changing with the times as public vehicles became motorised and ending up in the 1950s as a bus and coach operator.

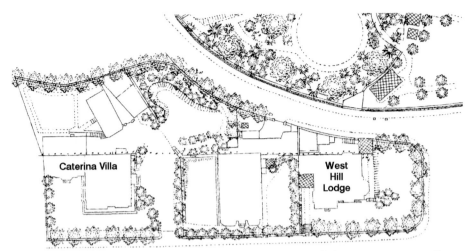

The villa circa 1875. Miss Moore's bedroom window was just beneath the 'Cat' in Caterina Villa.

Digression: Turf Hyland, John Swinard and Eliza Dansey Mushet

Elizabeth Dansey Mushet, née Bonsili, was the daughter of the Prince of Gomma, Abyssinia. When she was eighteen she met William Mushet, a wealthy, twenty-eight-year-old English yachtsman. After they wed in Malta in 1841 he brought her to England, where she was treated as an exotic novelty because of her skin colour. They moved to St Leonards in the hope that the sea air would cure her of consumption, but she died on 13th March 1845 and was interred in a vault beneath St Leonard's chapel.

Turf Hyland, aged nineteen, was one of a small gang besmirching the reputation of the new town of St Leonards. Hearing rumours that African women were 'buried in their jewels', and that the Abyssinian princess wore a silver crown to her grave, on 24th March he and two other hoodlums took a pickaxe and two crowbars and broke into the vault. Her casket, which was lined with lead and bricked-in, then encased in York stone, was smashed and torn open, but there were no jewels. Worse, they desecrated her body, placed a pillow on her face and pulled her dress up to the waist, 'and the body of the deceased was exposed'. The judge referred to their carrying out other disgusting acts, 'of such a nature as I cannot trust my tongue to mention'. They ripped the collection boxes off the walls and stole 1s 1d, drank a quarter-bottle of communion wine and left 'traces of revolting and almost incredible beastliness' by defecating in a glass tumbler.

When questioned by magistrates, Hyland 'behaved in a most coarse and disgusting manner'. Asked if he could read and write he replied, 'No, but I can *wrong* as well as anybody.' The charges against him were dismissed, but his partner in crime John Swinard, a twenty-one-year-old shoemaker with two previous convictions, was tried for sacrilege and theft. He was transported to Van Diemen's Land (Tasmania) for fourteen years, and died there two years later, aged twenty-five.

Turf led a life of crime: from 1849 to 1860 he was convicted seven times, always for theft, and served terms of between a week and six months in Lewes Gaol. In 1860 he received four years, and died a year after his release.

After being interrogated, Pearson was remanded for a week. The press revealed that 'his alarming situation has plunged all connected with him into the deepest grief'. Pearson himself was 'undismayed' because he had a solid alibi: at the time of the attack he was several miles away, walking between Battle and Silverhill, and he could produce plenty of witnesses to prove it.

Constable Sheather continued his diligent forensic investigation. He found a remarkably clear set of bootprints in the grounds of Caterina Villa. The heel of the right boot was worn down and had a half-pelt on the heel and an iron tip on the right toe, which had been broken in a unique pattern. He tracked the prints two miles north until they terminated, forty yards short of the Victoria Inn on Battle Road. He picked up the trail again in a shaw,[1] followed it for twelve yards, lost it, and then regained it close to the Victoria Inn. He was certain that the bootprints matched those found at Caterina Villa.

Sheather visited Hastings Gaol and pulled Pearson's Wellingtons off his feet. Only the heel of the right boot was worn down. It bore a half-pelt on the heel and an iron tip on the right toe, broken in an unusual fashion. Accompanied by Constable George Burgess and chemist George Johnson (as an independent, educated witness), Sheather took the Wellingtons to the locations of the prints. They fitted exactly. In one field there were fourteen prints that matched them. They searched around for Miss Moore's valuables but found nothing.

Local people, appalled by the murder of an innocent, defenceless female and doubtless spurred on by the £100 reward, were keen to help. On 17th November James Ashdown, a sawyer living in Hollington, continued Sheather's work in tracking the unique bootprints. He found some which led to a young ash tree, whose green bark looked 'as if some person had gnawed it with his teeth'. Thinking it might be a reminder of where something was buried, he swept away the dead leaves around it and, under an old whitethorn stub, three feet from the ash, he found a large, dark blue handkerchief, with a white border and spots, wrapped around a quantity of jewellery. He asked Jesse Hack, landlord of the Victoria Inn, to saw off the ash tree, which was later handed to Inspector Campbell when he arrived to take possession of the valuables.

The items were identified as Miss Moore's. They included seals and crests, watches, rings, bracelets and necklaces made of gold, emerald, topaz, diamonds and pearls; an amethyst brooch with a pendant heart 'thrown from Mount Vesuvius' and an old Pinchbeck watch. The total value of the items was between £100 and £250 (£10,000–£25,000 today).

Word got out that Pearson would be re-examined on Monday 20th November, and by 11am Hastings Town Hall was packed to capacity, whilst the High Street 'thronged with an excited multitude'. It was announced that proceedings would be conducted in private. The crowd hung around outside for a while, speculating on the case, then left.

1 A narrow coppice running like a hedgerow from the road between two fields.

At Pearson's third examination by magistrates, on Friday 24th November, the public was finally admitted. The bench included Mayor Alfred Burton (son of James Burton, the founder of St Leonards), Irishman Dr Peter McCabe[1] and Frederick Ticehurst. Others present included Pearson's solicitor J.G. Langham[2] and Captain Mackay, Chief Constable of East Sussex Constabulary. The town hall was 'crowded inside, and besieged outside by a dense and excited throng during the whole of the morning ... The rush at the opening of the hall doors was tremendous, and the body of the Court was speedily crowded to suffocation'.

When Pearson was placed in the dock 'his countenance wore an expression of anxiety'. Everyone's eyes fixed on him. They had never seen a murderer before. He was 5ft 7in, with a fresh complexion, red hair and whiskers, betraying his maternal Gaelic ancestry. Pearson initially appeared 'pale and downcast', he later 'recovered his self-possession' and even smiled once or twice. 'Since his imprisonment he is said to have manifested much levity of conduct,' wrote one reporter, adding: 'There is certainly none on this occasion. His manner was firm; and as the fresh witnesses were examined, and the depositions already taken were read over, he was an attentive listener'.

The next day Pearson was moved to Lewes House of Correction to await trial at the next assizes. A rumour that he would arrive by train from St Leonards at 11am caused a crowd to congregate at Lewes station. The train arrived but he failed to alight, so they hung around and were eventually joined by at least half the population of Lewes. Finally, with irons on his wrists and ankles and Hastings gaol keeper James Wellerd[3] close by his side, Pearson emerged from a train. Police attempted to hold back the baying mob, but it was impossible to get Pearson through. They sneaked him out via a side gate, but the crowd 'soon got on the scent and accompanied the police and their prisoner by foot all the way to the gaol.' Pearson was 'in excellent spirits, evincing a levity by no means in accordance with the gravity of his position'.

From his cell Pearson composed a letter to his parents, claiming himself 'as innocent of the crime imputed to him as his Maker is of sin'.

His trial was held on 22nd March 1849, from 9am until nearly midnight. The judge was the Rt Hon Sir James Parke, Bart; Mr Clarkson and Mr Horne appeared for the prosecution and Mr Ballantine for the defence. Pearson was indicted for 'having feloniously, wilfully, and of malice aforethought, struck, cut and wounded Mary Ann Newman with a spade, thereby giving her divers mortal wounds on the head, of which she died'. In the dock Pearson burst into tears and when called to plead asserted: 'I am as innocent as a child unborn'.

---

1. Dr McCabe was a former mayor. In the 1870s he discovered a chalybeate spring in just south of Buckshole Reservoir, which was known for many years as Dr McCabe's Spring.
2. James George Langham (1793–1877) was known as the 'smugglers' lawyer' because he often defended them in court and was (reputedly) paid in casks of brandy. He was an uncle of S.F. Langham, the coroner who conducted the inquest into the death of Jack the Ripper victim Catherine Eddowes.
3. Gaol keeper James Wellerd was murdered by a prisoner in 1856; the assailant was hanged.

His story was related to the court. After being dismissed by Miss Moore, Pearson had lodged with a washerwoman in Fulham. On Saturday 11th November she laundered his shirt front and white cravat whilst he washed his blue handkerchief himself. He intended to take a train from London Bridge to Tunbridge Wells, then walk to Hastings (the line to Hastings via Battle was under construction). Pearson could have used a different route to St Leonards (via Polegate) but that cost even more and he only managed to afford a ticket to Tunbridge Wells by begging a shilling.

Pearson said he left London by the 5pm train and slept in a stable loft at the George Inn at Tonbridge. Starting at 4am he walked the thirty miles to Hastings via Hurst Green, Robertsbridge and Battle. Between 12.30pm and 1pm he stopped for a few minutes each at the Victoria Inn and Tivoli Tollgate, then continued south to his parents' home in Hastings.

Ann was assaulted between 11.10am and 12.45pm. According to Pearson, at that time he was between Battle and Tivoli. He was definitely at the Victoria Inn at 12.45pm. The landlord and his wife testified that he came in, agitated, thirsty and broke, so they gave him a free tankard of water, which he 'gulped down'. Pearson's former boss, fly proprietor Thomas Skinner, also saw him, and he was certain it was between 12.40pm and 12.50pm. Although these were excellent witnesses, they did not see whether Pearson arrived from the south (having just killed Ann) or from the north (en route between Battle and Hastings).

The police produced their own witnesses. John Prior was hawking on Battle Road. Just south of the inn, at about noon, a man dressed 'like a gentleman's servant' passed him, going north. Pearson habitually wore a frock coat, striped trousers, shirt and cravat — the uniform of an upper servant. Mark Mepham, the miller at Tivoli, had a drink with a pal at the Victoria Inn, walked with him about three-quarters of a mile north up Battle Road, then turned back and headed south to Tivoli Gate. He did not see Pearson until about 1pm, when

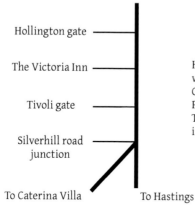

To Battle, Robertsbridge and Tunbridge Wells

Hollington gate ————

The Victoria Inn ————

Tivoli gate ————

Silverhill road junction ————

To Caterina Villa

To Hastings

Hollington Gate was located at the junction with (present-day) Telford Road and Tivoli Gate at the junction with (present-day) Paynton Road. Both were abolished in 1875. The Victoria Inn was rebuilt in the 1930s and is now a Co-Operative food store.

Pearson was cadging a drink of water at Tivoli Gate. The toll collectors, Mr and Mrs Daw, corroborated Mepham's testimony. Pearson mentioned paying 4s 6d for a third-class ticket to Tunbridge Wells. Later, a railway official stated that there was no 4s 6d fare in any class. A third-class ticket was 3s 4d.

Pearson's claim to have spent Saturday night at Tonbridge then set out at 4am to walk to Hastings was refuted by Hurst Green postman William Laurence. At 10pm on Saturday he chatted to Pearson by the gates of Iridge Place, halfway between Tunbridge Wells and Hastings. Pearson told him he had walked from London, sleeping overnight at Sevenoaks. He was thirsty and tired but had only a halfpenny. Laurence treated him to a pint pot of ale and two pipes of tobacco at the White Horse at Silver Hill, near Salehurst, after which they walked to Robertsbridge together, parting at midnight. Pearson did not give his name but mentioned knowing Yates, landlord of the Royal Oak, and Laurence recognised him as the man in the dock.

Evidence that bootprints at Caterina Villa matched those at Hollington was given by Sheather, Burgess, Hack, Johnson and Ashdown, the latter also described finding Miss Moore's valuables wrapped in a blue handkerchief.

Jane Cannon, James Grey, the washerwoman and Mrs Pearson each testified that the handkerchief in which the stolen goods were found resembled one of Pearson's: it was blue cotton with a white border. Grey recalled that Pearson's had a hole in it, as did the one used to hold the stolen goods.

Mrs Pearson said John had arrived as she was preparing lunch. It must have been before 1pm, as her husband had not yet returned from a booking for a bath-chair customer from 11am to 1pm. She gave John a meal and he asked for blacking and brushes to clean his muddy Wellingtons. He changed his linen (shirt front, stockings and cravat), leaving the soiled set behind, and asked for a clean handkerchief, saying he had lost the blue one she had given him.

Master cordwainer Stephen Brooker knew Pearson and the Moores. One of his workmen had repaired Pearson's right Wellington, using a pelt and a tip.

Looking west towards West Hill Road. The columns on the left are the Assembly Rooms. The building on the right is the eastern corner of South Lodge, where Brooker claimed to have stood when he saw Pearson in the archery ground on the brow of the hill.

On Sunday 12th November, whilst standing by the South Lodge entrance to St Leonards Gardens, he spotted Pearson standing sixty yards ahead, on the archery ground, seven yards from Miss Moore's stable. Emil Grosslob was smoking a pipe in his back garden at 3 West Ascent. He did not see Pearson but he did speak to Brooker and they watched the Moores' carriage pass them. This puts the time at about 10.35am. According to Pearson, at that time he was walking from Battle to Silverhill.

Ann gave testimony from the grave via Sarah Noakes, a former maid at Caterina Villa. Ann had told her of a nightmare in which Pearson and Hyland climbed into her ground floor bedroom window.

> I said to John, 'I know you, though you have tarred your face'. I said, 'don't hurt your mistress or me; take what you want, but don't hurt us'. When Pearson went to strike me with something like a spade, I screamed out and that awoke me.

Later, when Pearson was in the passage by the kitchen, Ann joked, 'Here comes that John Pearson, who is to kill me'. She must have told him about her dream because he replied, 'Ah, cook, if you do not die until I kill you with a spade you will live long enough'. On another occasion Ann told him: 'It's no use coming here, John, there is nothing for you'. He replied, 'Isn't there, I know what there is', adding that he didn't need anyone to tell him where to find it.

Gaol keeper Wellerd deposed that when Pearson's clothing was taken from him, he had remarked that 'Jack Ketch will have them'. Ketch was a 17th century public executioner; Pearson was alluding to the common belief that hangmen were allowed to retain the criminal's clothes. In other words, Pearson was expecting to be hanged, surely an admittance of guilt.

After nine hours of testimony and cross examination, the case against Pearson was cast-iron. He knew the layout and the domestic routine of Caterina Villa; he bore a grudge against Ann; he was seen lurking nearby just before she was attacked; the bootprints matched his exactly; and the stolen goods were found wrapped in a handkerchief identical to one he owned but could not produce. The independent witnesses found by the police proved that Pearson had lied about his whereabouts before, during and after the murder.

At 6pm defence counsel William Ballantine began his 'energetic address'. It occupied nearly three hours, during which he disparaged everything every witness had said. There was nothing but circumstantial evidence, and history books were full of people who had been hanged on such evidence and later found to be innocent. He argued that witnesses were 'coloured by' the hope of getting a portion of the reward, and appealed to the jury for an acquittal.

The judge's summing up lasted two-and-a-half hours. He ordered the jury to form a judgment solely from the evidence. If it left the question doubtful, it was their duty to acquit. By then it was nearly midnight and the trial had dragged on for almost fifteen hours. The jury took just five minutes to return a

Mr W. Ballantine in 1844. *Illustrated London News.*
John Pearson being questioned at Hastings police
court. *Sussex Advertiser.*

verdict of 'not guilty'. Pearson was then quickly arraigned on an indictment of robbery. He pleaded not guilty and was again acquitted.

The investigation was closed because there was no other suspect. Everyone knew Pearson was guilty but, as one reporter put it, Ballantine had 'wheedled' an acquittal out of the jury. Another referred to 'The strange verdicts of juries', and *The Times* called it 'startling in the extreme' and wondered if 'Not guilty' was a typographical error. *The Era* was certain Pearson did it, and argued that hanging him was kinder than condemning him to a life burdened with guilt:

> He cannot leave his conscience in the dock; he cannot forget himself or make the world forget him. Who would not rather be dead and buried than the living John Pearson? Repentance and contrition — the agony of remorse, and the consciousness of public loathing, are all fearful to contemplate.

However, Pearson's subsequent life shows that being tried for murder did not scupper his chances of marriage, nor did it deter employers or landlords. Moreover, instead of contrition and repentance, his future was characterised by robbery, violence and revenge.

In 1851 Pearson married Harriet Jones and was hired by Charles Pope Hutchings, the highly respected owner of the classy Marine Hotel at Pelham Place. Hutchings kept fourteen horses and a dozen carriages in stables and coachhouses in Wellington Mews, above which Pearson lived, alongside several other fly drivers and coachmen.

Pearson was summoned in 1858 for assaulting a lad of fourteen, but he bribed the boy's father, a fellow flyman, not to prosecute. Two years later, during a row with a colleague, Pearson seized a pitchfork and struck the man over the knuckles. After working for Mr Hutchings for thirteen years Pearson robbed him of a large quantity of oats and straw, for which he served twelve months with hard labour. When released his first act was to go after the main prosecution witness, William Elphick. He stormed into the Denmark Arms 'in a pugilistic fashion', threw his cap into the air and announced his intention to give Elphick 'a good thrashing', adding that he would 'Lay wait for him and do for him'. Elphick genuinely feared for his life. Even Pearson's solicitor, J.G. Langham, admitted that 'what he might do when he lost his temper it was impossible to say'. Pearson was charged with using threatening language and bound over in the sum of £20. In 1866 he appeared on the 'wanted' list of the *Police Gazette* for stealing a horse. A warrant was issued for his arrest and he went on the run. Eventually he was apprehended and sentenced to three months with hard labour.

Despite his propensity for theft and violence, let alone having been tried for murder, people seemed perfectly happy to employ Pearson as a fly driver and to rent him accommodation (over the next few years he lived variously at 7 Brook Street, 4 Waldegrave Street and 18 Russell Street). He died in 1880, aged fifty-five. His widow survived him but they had no children.

Epilogue: Ann Newman, the Moores and Caterina Villa

Ann Newman's final resting place was the burial ground of the Wesleyan Methodist chapel in Norman Road. Built in 1836, it was destroyed by fire in 1900. In 1900 the *HSLO* published a lengthy article about its history, which included a section about Miss Newman:

THE CHAPEL GRAVEYARD.

It may not be known to the majority of townspeople that at the side of the Chapel there are several gravestones erected to the sacred memory of those whose remains were placed beneath ... When the enlargement of the Chapel took place a considerable portion of the graveyard was utilised for the purposes of extension, and the graves were all concreted over. It is pleasing to know that the stones which remain outside the church have not been damaged by the fire. There are altogether twelve stones ... [which] stand against the wall on the west side of the church ... One stone recalls the sad end of a young [sic] servant girl and it is notable for its quaint inscription. Many stones have so decayed that the inscriptions are not discernible, but on the particular stone just mentioned, which is in a fair state of preservation, the beholder is informed that

> HERE ARE DEPOSITED
> THE MANGLED REMAINS OF POOR
> M.A. NEWMAN,
>
> WHO WAS BARBAROUSLY MURDERED BY A
> MISCREANT ON THE 12TH NOVEMBER 1848, AND
> WHO AFTERWARDS PLUNDERED THE HOUSE,
> BUT WHO AS YET HAS ESCAPED PUNISHMENT,
> BUT HER BLOOD STILL CRIETH FOR
> VENGEANCE, AND HE WHOSE LAWS CANNOT
> BE BROKEN WITH IMPUNITY HAS SAID:
>
> 'WHOSO SHEDDETH MAN'S BLOOD,
> BY MAN SHALL HIS BLOOD BE SHED.'

'It appears', concluded the *HSLO*, 'that a man was arrested, but was acquitted on a technicality, and lived in the town several years after'.

It is hard to imagine the genteel Miss Moore using the term 'mangled remains', but she must have approved it, for she would have paid for the headstone. She could afford the best quality materials and the most skilled stonemason, which is perhaps why Ann's headstone fared better over time than others. The chapel was rebuilt in 1900 in Gothic style and was in use for just over a century; however, the congregation dwindled until it was no longer viable. After it closed in 2005 it was converted into five flats, using a sympathetic architectural design that retains both its facade and its elegant spire.

In 1854 Miss Moore offered Caterina Villa for sale, but received no offers. She and her brother lived there until their deaths, in 1858 and 1860 respectively. After changing hands several times the villa, renamed 'Davenham' and later 'Fairhaven', was bought by Herbert Hardinge, a literary hanger-on best known as the gay lover of the renowned reciter Clifford Harrison.[1] In 1907 Hardinge invited the famous novelist Marie Corelli to stay with him for a week, and set up a writing desk especially for her in a ground floor room overlooking the garden. Here, according to the *HSLO*, she 'wrote the murder scene of her new novel'. Sadly, the report did not reveal if Miss Corelli knew about the gruesome murder committed one storey beneath her, half a century previously.

Eventually Caterina Villa and its outbuildings were converted into flats and renamed West Hill Court. It is a Grade II listed building.

References: *South Eastern Gazette* 8th April 1845; *Sussex Advertiser* 21st & 28th November 1848; 1st April 1849, 27th March 1849 & 25th December 1849; *Brighton Gazette* 30th November 1848 & 29th March 1849; *Morning Post* 15th & 20th November 1848; *The Times* 20th November 1848 & 26th March 1849; *The Era* 1st April 1849; *HSLO* 21st April 1900, 9th November 1907; 2nd September 1916.

1. Reciters gave public readings from books, using perfect diction. Harrison lived and died at Osborne House in Ore.

Caterina Villa in 2019. The ground floor bay window on the far left was Miss Moore's room. *Below*: its Tudor charm is evident in this recent photo of the original porch.

Digression: Emil Grosslob

One of the minor witnesses at Pearson's trial was Emil Christian Grosslob (1797–1867). A native of Saxony, he had been a publisher in London but went bankrupt and in 1837 ended up in a debtor's prison. By 1841 he and his wife had moved to Hastings.

In 1848 he discovered a chalybeate spring in the north part of the grounds of his home at 3 West Ascent. He spent a large sum erecting guest accommodation, Russian baths and a pump room, and named it St Leonards Spa. In 1853 the novelist George Eliot stayed there. Her lover, George Lewes. was writing a biography of Goethe and was curious about Grosslob's claim to have known him years before in his native Germany.

The spa was destroyed by fire in 1864 and Grosslob built Turkish baths on the site. After his death they were rebuilt again in 1871 by a new owner. Later they became a school's swimming pool. The building was converted into a residential bungalow, which is currently for sale at £1.25m.

Left: the new frontage of the baths, built in 1871.

The White Hart at Guestling.

The Eatons' grocery shop opposite the Geerings' cottage.

1848 • 1849

The Family Poisoner

Guestling

Mary Ann Plumb was baptised at St Andrew's, Fairlight, on 21st July 1799. She was the fourth child of Sarah Anscomb, who had two children in her teens before marrying illiterate farm labourer George Plumb in 1797. According to Mary Ann, her mother 'learned me to read at home, and was always careful to teach me, but my father had no knowledge to teach.' As a child she minded her eight younger siblings so both parents could work, but after she secretly pawned several articles of others' clothing and pocketed the money she was packed off into domestic service at nearby Old Coghurst Farm.

Whilst there she became pregnant by farmhand Richard Geering; she was sixteen; he was twenty-one. She was sacked and her parents insisted she marry him. Mary Ann announced defiantly 'No man shall rule me!' but she eventually bowed to pressure, because 'My father and mother over-persuaded me'. On her wedding day she had to be 'carried into church'.

Richard's family came from Tarring Neville. When he was four they moved to Hastings, where his sister married Richard Beany and his brother James became licensee of a beer-shop in East Street that is now the London Trader.

Mary Ann and Richard married on 27th December 1816 at the church of St Mary & St Peter in Pett.[1] They and both their witnesses were illiterate and so all signed the register with an X-shaped mark.

Over the next twenty-five years Mary Ann gave birth to two girls and eight boys. Most were born between 1817 and 1836 at Harmer's Cottages, Westfield.[2] The family moved to Guestling, where Andrew was born in December 1839 and Peter in March 1842.

The Geerings' cottage at Guestling Green was situated at the end of a row of five in a terrace known as the Long House. There was one room upstairs and two downstairs, but fortunately by the time the youngest were born the eldest had left: Jane took a job as a domestic servant in London, married and stayed there; James was a waggoner for Sir John Ashburnham;[3] Alban worked as a house servant to farmer John Hoad at Icklesham and William moved out after his wife had their first child.

1. The building no longer exists, as the church was rebuilt in 1864.
2. Births before 1837 were not registered; here are their baptismal dates: Jane, April 1817; William, April 1820; James, December 1822; Alban, May 1825; George, August 1827; Benjamin, May 1831; Edwin, October 1833; Mary, April 1836.
3. Sir John was the rector of Guestling church for sixty years until 1854.

The Geering children learned basic reading, writing and arithmetic thanks to Robert Bradshaw, a former rector of Pett and Guestling, who had bequeathed land and funds for a two-roomed school.[1] Borrowing her children's copybooks, Mary Ann added elementary writing to her basic reading skills.

The family was very hardworking. Father and sons laboured on farms; mother and daughter took care of the family's domestic needs, a tough life indeed before the days of sanitation, running water, gas and electricity. Feeding hungry farm workers on a tight budget was a struggle, and meals were simple, cheap and repetitive: mainly bread, butter, cheese, eggs and the occasional rabbit pie or meat pudding. To keep the family afloat Mary Ann began to walk to Hastings every Monday to pawn their Sunday best, then she would buy it back every Saturday when her menfolk received their weekly wages.

Mary Ann and Richard were both by nature quick-tempered and argumentative. They squabbled throughout their married life and, as she reached middle age, Mary Ann's hostility became habitual and blatant: neighbours heard her say 'scores of times' that she wished her husband dead.

In middle age one of the couple inherited £20 (about half a year's wages). By law anything inherited by either spouse was the husband's property, and in January 1846 Richard decided unilaterally to deposit the windfall in the Hastings Savings Bank. Mary Ann was annoyed, believing that they ought to use it to clear their debts. She later explained:

> The boys were out of work now and then, and we were often at a loss to make both ends meet. People kept coming for their money; they knew that twenty pounds had been left us, and was in the Savings Bank, but he would not have it touched.

In March 1847 Richard asked his sister to withdraw £5 for him and to retain the book to prevent his wife from accessing any of the remaining £15. This infuriated Mary Ann. A few months later she wreaked revenge: she casually asked her sister-in-law for the book on the pretext that her son Alban 'wanted to look it over'. She kept it, and over the next few months secretly withdrew £14 18s 8d, leaving just one shilling and fourpence.

By the summer of 1848 nine people were living in the cottage. Richard and Mary Ann, Andrew, Peter and Mary slept upstairs, whilst George, Ben, James and Edwin slept downstairs. The nine became thirteen after William's wife died in September 1848, because he moved back home with his three small children, paying his mother nine shillings a week to feed the four of them.[2]

From July Richard, then fifty-three, developed stomach trouble. One day in September, whilst working at Fish Ponds Farm, he twice threw up after eating a packed lunch his wife had prepared. Two days later the same thing happened at home. He recovered and, three days later, it started again.

---

1. The school at Guestling is now called Guestling Bradshaw CE School.
2. One of them, James, appears in a chapter in Volume Two.

The Bradshaw Charity paid John Innes Pocock — 'surgeon and apothecary of Winchilsea' — £30 a year stipend to attend the rural poor.[1] Visiting Richard on Sunday 10th September, he found him suffering from 'chills, fever, cough, difficulty and pain on breathing, sickness, pain in the abdomen, and sweating.' He prescribed blue pill and colocynth, and a curious concoction comprising sulphuric acid, Epsom salts, sulphate of quinine and peppermint water.

When Ben arrived home at noon on Wednesday, 13th September he joined his mother and his brother George sitting at his father's bedside. Twenty minutes later Richard passed away.

Mr Pocock was sent for. He was astonished to find Richard had died, but Mary Ann said the Geerings had a hereditary heart defect. Despite having no verification of this fanciful story, and without a post mortem, Pocock issued a certificate attributing Richard's death to 'heart disease'.

Village nurse Judith Veness prepared the body for burial. 'The corpse was very black and much decayed,' she recalled, 'and the skin came off the back of his neck as it was placed in the coffin.' Carpenter George Hawkins had made the coffin, which was left open on a trestle in the ground floor room of the cottage for two days before he screwed down the lid.

Mary Ann pawned Richard's work smock and another article for 2s at Sarah Betts's shop in Hastings and asked her to make 'two gowns and two bonnets as mourning' for herself and her daughter. She collected them a few days later, but never paid Mrs Betts's invoice. Visiting Houghton's, at 95 All Saints' Street, she pawned Richard's fob watch, which he had left to their son Peter.

On 17th September Richard was interred in a grave on the east side of St Laurence church. At Mary Ann's request it was dug six feet deep instead of the usual four, and a heavy slab of wood was placed on top of the coffin. She asked gravedigger John Hawkins to apply to Sir John Ashburnham for a section of the burial ground to be reserved for her family to be interred together, and showed him a spot she had already selected.

Before there were state benefits or sick pay, 'friendly' or 'burial' societies existed throughout Britain, and the Geerings paid 1s a month into one based at the White Hart Inn. Each member was entitled to 1s 8d for each day they were too sick to work and 10s a week for long-term illness. There were roughly a hundred members, and when one died the rest chipped in a shilling for the funeral. The day Richard died Mary Ann applied for and received 3s 4d for two days' sick pay, plus £4 18s for the funeral (which actually cost her £2 5s).

After the burial everyone gathered at the cottage for afternoon tea. Mary Ann announced that Richard did not want the savings bank money touched for twelve months, then it must be divided equally between his family. It was merely a ruse to buy herself time, because she had almost emptied the account. A month later she blatantly lied to Alban, saying there was £12 left.

1. The same Dr Pocock who appears in 'Life and Sole'.

In December twenty-one-year-old George became ill. He was bedridden for weeks, with a raging thirst and repeated bouts of intense vomiting. James, then twenty-six, shared the round-the-clock nursing duties with his mother. George repeatedly rallied, then relapsed, until he expired on 27th December. Mr Pocock gave the cause of death as 'fever'. Six weeks after George's funeral it was James's turn. He died on 6th March 1849; according to the death certificate, this time it was 'gastritis'. Mary Ann made two more successful claims to the Guestling Friendly Society and added two more coffins to the graveyard.

All three had suffered the same symptoms, yet Mr Pocock issued certificates stating three different, and unrelated, causes of death. In addition, although in just six months three fit and strong men in one household had died, he failed to raise any concerns with the coroner.

The deaths left only four in the house: Mary Ann, Edwin, Ben and Mary. The vacant space was soon filled when William and his three children, who had moved out for a while, returned. Clearly, he did not suspect foul play.

A month after James died, on Good Friday, 6th April, Mary Ann made her first attempt at poisoning eighteen-year-old Ben. Her second was on Easter Sunday. After feeding his master's bullocks, Ben went home for breakfast and, shortly after sharing a pot of tea with his mother, felt 'sick as death' and threw up green vomit. Like the others, he took to his bed.

Mary Ann told neighbours that a fortune teller had predicted that she would 'lose her husband and the greater part of her family within three years', then pretended to fear that it was coming true. Three had gone, and now Ben was ill. They urged her to fetch Mr Ticehurst, a senior physician who, when he was Pocock's predecessor under Bradshaw's Charity, had gained the trust and respect of everyone for miles around.[1]

On 11th April Mary Ann loitered outside Mr Ticehurst's at 41 High Street until he emerged. At her request he called on Ben two days later. Finding the boy gravely ill, the doctor issued strict orders of nil by mouth except for water. He later discovered that Mary Ann had given him ginger beer and a cup of milk. On Sunday 15th both Ticehurst and Pocock visited Ben, bringing an array of potions and powders. When Mr Ticehurst returned six days later Ben answered the door, fully recovered. He mentioned that he had already made a claim for sick pay and handed the cash to his mother.

The following Saturday Mary Ann baked a loaf, which she and Ben enjoyed for lunch with a helping of butter and cheese, washed down with coffee. Ben was ill for three days. On 23rd April Mr Ticehurst took home a sample of Ben's green vomit. Marsh's test and Reinsch's test revealed that it contained arsenic.

Ticehurst and Pocock visited again and questioned both Ben and his mother. There had been no arsenic in the house for a year; Mary Ann no longer needed it to destroy rodents since acquiring a vigilant cat. Before Ben had fallen

1. Frederick Ticehurst (1810–1877) served Hastings for half a century as a surgeon, magistrate and alderman. He was mayor for five years and coroner for ten. He appears in other chapters.

ill she had partaken of the same food and drank tea from the same pot, and yet felt no ill effects. It was most baffling. Again vomit was taken away, and again tests proved positive for arsenic. This time Mr Ticehurst removed the lad from his mother and, after witnessing his speedy recovery, told the police his suspicions and wrote to Coroner Nathaniel Polhill Kell about the earlier deaths.

One of the Geerings' neighbours, Police Constable George Jeffery, was sent to investigate. He and Superintendent John Alexander Thompson conducted a thorough search of the Geerings' cottage. In a box in the upstairs room they found forty-nine duplicates (receipts for goods pawned) and a collection of medicine bottles, including one wrapped in paper with a label bearing the word 'poison'. It contained red precipitate, a crystalline form of mercuric oxide, used medicinally as an ointment for the treatment of chancre and various skin diseases. Mary Ann said it was 'for the children's heads ... for they are apt to get vermin when they go to school'. A large vial containing a viscid, yellowish liquid had been hidden in the garden. It turned out to be balsam capivi, the bitter oleoresin of several species of Copaifera, a genus of trees native to South America and the West Indies, used as a stimulant and diuretic.

Mary Ann was arrested at 6pm on 26th April and conveyed in a police cart to the watch-house on the ground floor of Hastings Town Hall, where she was charged with poisoning Ben. Her youngest children Mary, Andrew and Peter — aged thirteen, nine and six — were taken into Guestling Workhouse.

An inquest on all three of the deceased was held over four sessions: 27th April and 2nd, 3rd and 17th May at the White Hart Inn, half a mile uphill from the Geerings' home. At the first session the jury viewed the corpses at St Laurence church. On the warrant of Coroner Kell the coffins had been disinterred and awaited examination by Mr Ticehurst, assisted by Mr Pocock

Hastings Police in 1854 outside their first station, within the town hall in the High Street.

St Laurence church, Guestling.

Guestling Green in 1873.

and two other surgeons: Walter Duke of 46 George Street and John Savery of 12 York Buildings.[1]

Richard's coffin was placed on a tombstone and the lid unscrewed. His corpse was in an advanced state of decomposition. 'The effluvium was dreadful, and the body swimming in water. The smell arising therefrom was most nauseous'. Mr Ticehurst cut into the torso and removed several organs, placing them into carefully-labelled glass jars. He did the same with the other two victims, then took the jars, plus one containing Ben's vomit, to Guy's Hospital, London, and handed them to Professor Alfred Swaine Taylor, the country's foremost analytical chemist.[2]

The inquest was adjourned awaiting medical reports. Foreman Thomas Arkcoll and the other jury members were required to enter into their own recognizances in the sum of £10 to ensure their attendance at the next session.

The story — described as 'an extraordinary sensation' — began to appear in newspapers across Britain. One reporter revealed that 'the minds of the inhabitants ... have been thrown into a dreadful state of excitement from circumstances of a painful and shocking character.' Should poisoning be proved, the case would be 'one of the most appalling circumstances that ever took place in this part of the country'. When word got out that Mary Ann was to be brought to the office of John Goldsworthy Shorter,[3] town clerk and clerk to the magistrates:

1. John Savery MD (1799–1873) was in practice here for fifty years; his son, John Charles (1830–1874), also a physician, appears in the chapter 'Three Men Down'.
2. Professor Taylor became known as 'the father of British forensic medicine'.
3. As coroner, Mr Shorter appears in the earlier chapter 'The Cook of Caterina Villa'.

A large number of the inhabitants assembled in High street for the purpose of obtaining a glance at the supposed perpetrator of the horrid crime ... but she having been brought to the office at least half an hour before the time specified, the majority were disappointed. Nevertheless, the crowd did not disperse, but the contrary. At the close of the examination the number was considerably augmented, and at last, they succeeded in having their curiosity gratified. Mrs Geering is a short but rather stout person, with something very repulsive in her appearance, particularly smooth-tongued in her expressions, and perfectly confident in her manner.

Mary Ann 'denied her guilt, said she loved her husband and children, and called upon the Almighty to bear witness to her innocence'. She wrote a letter to her children but it was intercepted by the gaoler and given to the magistrates, who retained it as evidence against her. The contents were read out in court and later published in the press. Whilst not overtly confessing to murder she admitted buying arsenic and other poisons, mixing them together and baking them in the oven to make a bolus. She regretted not saving some poison to take herself.

Constable Jeffery searched the cottage again and found a large bolus wrapped in paper and tucked inside a chest of drawers. 'It was not like a doctor's pill but seemed to be a home-made one', he remarked. Mr Ticehurst sent it to Professor Taylor to be analysed, along with some other curious drugs and mysterious liquids.

Over the following days the full story emerged from the mouths of witnesses during hearings in the magistrates' court and at the inquests. These were always crowded to capacity with neighbours, townspeople, civic officials, legal men, medical men, police, gentry and farmers.

Professor Taylor's analysis confirmed that the bolus contained arsenic and opium. The effect of opium was to deaden pain and check vomiting. Richard and James had died of poisoning by arsenic, and George had been killed with mercury.

Eli West Stubbs, a druggist in Hastings since 1826, said that Mrs Geering had purchased arsenic from him on three occasions in 1848, saying she needed it to kill rats and mice. Each time she had requested a penny-worth, which was about a dram, or between 40 and 60 grains. Mr Stubbs always hand-labelled it 'arsenic-poison'. 'Mrs Geering and my assistant were always joking together', he recalled, 'and in July 1848 he lent her a sovereign. She never came into the shop again. He was always ashamed to mention that he had lent a sovereign to a female.'[1]

1. She wasn't the last poisoner to obtain her deadly supplies from a Hastings druggist. Half a century later George Chapman followed suit and also killed three people. He was later suspected of the Whitechapel Murders. See Helena Wojtczak (2017) *Jack the Ripper at Last?*

From mid-1848 Mary Ann began to obtain arsenic from Henry Pittman at The Creek, buying a penny-worth four times. The system of signing a register had yet to be introduced, but he later recalled the approximate dates of her purchases and they coincided with the weeks before each of the deaths.

Gossip spread that Mary Ann's motive was financial, specifically that she killed to obtain Friendly Society payouts. She had claimed 10s a week for three weeks whilst George was ill and, on the day he died, she received £4 16s funeral benefit. When James died his two days' sick pay, at 1s 8d a day, and £4 18s for the funeral, were also paid to her. His coffin and funeral fees amounted to £2 14s, so from each death Mary Ann pocketed about £2, the equivalent of two weeks' wages. In addition, she profited from selling their belongings: she had secretly pawned two watches, three frocks, three jackets, four pairs of trousers, three waistcoats and a neckerchief. Lastly, Mr Bishop, actuary of the Hastings Savings Bank, stated that during 1847–48, Mary Ann had withdrawn nearly all of Richard's money, leaving just 1s 4d.

After what the press called 'a painful investigation, almost unparalleled in the criminal annals of this country', the coroner's jury returned three verdicts of 'wilful murder' and Mary Ann was committed to the House of Correction at Lewes to await trial. By then the case was nationally famous, partly because *The Times* had published six news reports about the murders. Soon, the story began to appear in the American and Australian newspapers.

The trial took place on 7th August 1849 at Lewes Crown Court. The judges were the Lord Chief Baron Sir Frederick Pollock and Mr Baron Alderson. Twenty-two men were sworn in as a Grand Jury, and numerous dignitaries, magistrates, mayors, coroners and lawyers from across the county came to watch.

Mary Ann was placed at the bar and four indictments were read out to her: three counts of murder and one attempt to destroy a life. To each charge she replied firmly, 'I am not guilty'. She was then tried for the murder of her husband. Mr Horne and Mr Creasy conducted the prosecution. They and the judges had no qualms about allowing a trial that could result in the death penalty to be held without the accused having any defence counsel.

When the third prosecution witness, Ben Geering, took the stand his eldest sibling Jane, now Mrs Broom, came forward. She had travelled from London to engage counsel for her mother, but had no means to pay. Several barristers had been approached for help *pro bono* but all had declined. In response the Lord Chief Baron asked one of the senior lawyers present, a Mr Hurst, to 'watch the case on behalf of the prisoner'.

There were no witnesses for the defence, and so the onus was on Mr Hurst to think up something to say in Mary Ann's favour. He pointed out the absence of motive. Clearly, it was not financial, since (he thought) all money gained went on burial expenses. He called 'most earnestly upon the jury to give the prisoner the benefit of any doubt that might suggest itself to their minds'.

The judge's summing up occupied two hours and ten minutes and was a reiteration of the prosecution's case. The jury knew that finding Mary Ann guilty meant she would be executed, yet they took less than ten minutes to reach that verdict. The Lord Chief Baron placed the black cap[1] upon his elaborate wig and entreated Mary Ann to make her peace with God. In his own words:

> Through the merits and mediation of our Saviour, to seek for salvation in the next world, for you have little chance of forgiveness in this. The sentence of the Court upon you is, that you be taken to the place from whence you came, and from thence to the place of execution, and that you be there hanged by the neck till you be dead, and that your body be buried within the precincts of the prison, where you shall be confined previous to your execution, and may God in His infinite mercy have compassion upon your soul.

According to the press, she 'appeared not in the least affected at her situation, and left the bar totally unmoved'.

Mr Hurst clutched at one final straw by submitting a written complaint objecting to a technical point relating to allowable evidence. A panel of judges briefly considered the matter before dismissing it. The execution would go ahead as scheduled: Mary Ann would be publicly hanged on 21st August.

During her eleven-day wait for death Mary Ann made a confession of guilt to the chaplain, Rev. Richard Burnet B.A.[2] She did it in stages, first telling him she had killed Richard, and later adding that she had poisoned her boys. 'The prisoner appearing penitent', explained one pressman, 'the chaplain conceived himself justified in administering to her the sacrament of the Lord's Supper'. Burnet later wrote up the 'sad and awful story' of her life and crimes in order to release it to the press after her execution. The part where she (supposedly) explained her motive to him read:

> The fact is, I am guilty of all. When I turned my back upon my husband, I turned my back upon God; and the devil drove me to that pitch of wickedness, that I determined to destroy all my family, and then myself. I was tired of the world, and wanted to get rid of it altogether; and I did not want to leave any of them behind me ... I expected to meet them in heaven. It was not done for money. If there was no money it would not have made any difference.

On 21st August 1849 a scaffold was erected within the outer yard at the southern end of the House of Correction, in an elevated position above the wall facing Little East Street.

---

1. The 'black cap' was a misnomer: it was a square of plain, black fabric, placed on top of the judicial wig. One of its four corners faced forward when a death sentence was pronounced.
2. Rev. Mr Burnet left Lewes about 1872 and was for a short time vicar of Christ Church, Ore.

The House of Correction was on the corner of Lancaster Street and North Street, Lewes, next to the present police station. Opened in 1793, in 1845 it became the County Gaol (or Jail) for Sussex. When the current prison was built in 1853 the old building was used to hold prisoners of war from Crimea. It later became a naval prison. The building was demolished in 1963.

By ten o'clock the numbers congregated in North-street. The gallows being plainly visible for a long distance both above and below the gaol, and throughout the length of Little East-street, various crowds took up their position at such different points as appeared to them to offer the best view of the proceedings ...

'As usual', opined one reporter, 'the crowd comprised the very scum of the population'.

By half-past eleven a vast crowd had assembled. The tolling of the death-bell, at stated intervals, gave indication how nearly the moment was approaching which would remove the unhappy object of the solemn ceremonies of the day from all connection with things worldly, and transfer her from trial and sentence on earth to be finally judged before the great tribunal of her Almighty and all-merciful Father.

As twelve o'clock struck, the sad procession made its appearance on the steps leading to the scaffold. Under-Sheriffs, Chaplain, Governor of the Prison. The wretched criminal Geering came next, supported up to the steps by two of the turnkeys, closely followed by Calcraft, the executioner, and two other officers of the gaol. Mary Ann Geering was dressed in a black gown and shawl, the latter having a coloured border. She wore neither bonnet nor cap, and the shawl was pinned close around the neck. On reaching the platform of the scaffold, the authorities ranged themselves around the unhappy woman. The Rev. Chaplain then read the solemn service appropriate to the occasion, whilst the executioner commenced the performance of his sad duties.

Having drawn a white nightcap over the head and face of the wretched woman the fatal cord was passed around her neck, the knot being placed immediately under the right ear. This being done and the rope having been made fast to the cross beam of the gallows, Calcraft descended the steps and in a second the fatal bolt was drawn, and the dark transgressor of the offended laws of her country was launched into eternity. On falling, her hands were closely clasped as if in earnest prayer, but after a second or two, they fell powerless by her side. A few conclusive struggles followed, and then the stillness of death told that life and feeling were extinct.

At one o'clock the body ... was cut down and handed over to the authorities for interment. The scaffold was then removed, thus leaving no trace behind of the painful ceremony of the day.

At 4 o'clock Mrs Geering was buried within the precincts of the gaol.
After her death, the press felt free to malign her more freely, claiming that even as a child she was 'noted for her cunning and double-facedness'. Her appearance was slated as 'masculine and forbidding', and her character as 'low

and grovelling, mixed up with a vast amount of sly cunning'. What is more, she was only poor because she was 'a gin drinker and a determined opium eater'.

Mary Ann Geering was the first of only two people executed at the old gaol at Lewes. Both were women, and the second was hanged three years later, in 1852. Sarah Ann French, known as 'the Onion Pie Murderer', had (supposedly) attended Mary Ann's execution and subsequently used arsenic to kill her own husband. The cases bore other similarities: Professor Taylor gave the forensic evidence and Mr Creasy prosecuted; both of the accused had no defence counsel and instead had her trial 'watched' by a *pro bono* lawyer randomly chosen. The women were attended by the same chaplain, hanged by the same executioner, buried in the same graveyard, and the coffins of both were later moved to the grounds of the new prison.

The pair were among the seventeen female murderers executed in the decade between 1843 and 1852. Poison was women's murder weapon of choice, and untold numbers got away with it because their crimes went undetected. Even some of those who were caught and tried were acquitted, for example Sarah Chesham, aka 'Sally Arsenic', who was found not guilty in the spring of 1847 of killing her two sons and an unrelated child.[1]

During the inquests into the deaths of the three Geerings, several people, including members of the jury, had pointed out that, had Mr Pocock realised early on that Richard was being poisoned, three lives might have been saved. (Actually, it was four: Mary Ann would not have been hanged.) The local Board of Guardians concurred and invited Mr Pocock to resign, stating that he 'no longer enjoyed the confidence of the Board'. Pocock stubbornly refused to 'do the gentlemanly thing', but the complaint against him was not sufficiently damning to justify dismissal.

Later in 1849 Mr Frederick Ticehurst was presented with a handsome gift from the people of Hastings & St Leonards, in recognition of his fine service to the public. It consisted of 100 guineas' worth of silver plate, and the valedictory inscription cited his work on the Guestling poisonings and acknowledged his key role in saving the life of young Benjamin Geering.

References: *John Bull* 25th & 27th August 1849; *Sussex Advertiser* 1st May 1849 & 30th October 1849; *Hastings & St Leonards News* 28th April 1849; *The Times* 29th April 1849; *Observer* 30th April 1849; *Lloyd's Weekly* 20th May 1849; *Bell's Life* 5th August 1849; *Morning Post* 22nd August 1849; *The Standard* 22nd August 1849; *The Patriot* 6th August 1849. *Hampshire Advertiser* 25th August 1849; *Blackburn Standard* 8th August 1849, and Mary Ann's confession, as written by the chaplain.

1. In 1851, two years after Mary Ann was executed, Mrs Chesham was also hanged for 'administering poison with intent to kill', which suggested that at her 1847 trial she had been wrongly acquitted. Her case led to the Sale of Arsenic Act, which introduced poisons' registers at the point of sale.

1849

CHAIR TRIGGER

ORE

North Row was a long, curved terrace of workers' cottages, halfway between the King's Head and the workhouse. Among its earliest residents were George and Ann Harman, a couple in their thirties who moved there from Guestling in 1846. They doubtless knew the Geering family (see previous chapter) and would have heard every grisly detail about the shocking murders from the family and friends they left behind.

In 1848 a band of navvies arrived in Ore to build a railway line between Hastings and Ashford, including a 1,400-yard tunnel under The Ridge. North Row was close to the site, making it an ideal place for them to lodge. Although married for five years the Harmans were still childless, and so had the room to take in a navvy. The precipitous hills and shifting sandstone and marl made that section of line exceedingly tricky to build and he lodged with them for more than a year.

By all accounts, the trio lived happily together. George Stone, who was twenty-two and a native of Kent, proved to be the ideal lodger: friendly, reliable, honest and ever willing to lend a hand or perform any chore.

George Harman was a stoker at Hastings gas works.[1] As a hobby he shot starlings, using an ancient shotgun with a rusty percussion lock. On Monday 22nd October 1849 he loaded but did not fire the gun. Leaving it standing upright in the corner of the parlour, at about 5pm, as he prepared to walk into Hastings to start his night shift, he told Ann to warn the lodger that it was loaded.

It appears that she forgot.

That evening George Stone arrived home from work. As usual Ann had prepared supper, which they ate sitting at opposite ends of the table. Afterwards she served a pot of tea. According to George:

> We were laughing and talking one with the other on different things betwixt us. She took the tea-tray off the table to clear away the tea. The gun was standing at my left hand. I moved the chair a little bit, and I took the gun in my right hand first, and my left hand was on the chair. As I lifted the gun up, the gun just touched the knob of the chair and instantly went off.

1. The works opened in 1830 to provide gas to the town's 82 street lamps. Morrisons supermarket now covers the site.

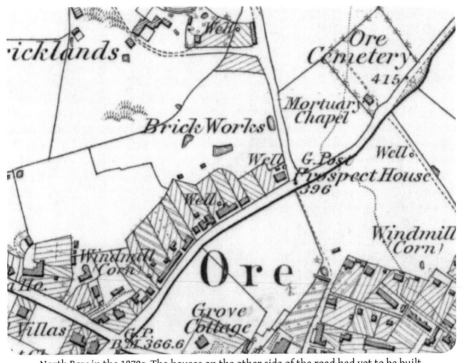

North Row in the 1870s. The houses on the other side of the road had yet to be built.

The shock of the unexpected and deafening explosion caused Stone to 'fall in a fit'. After a few minutes he came round and stood up. To his horror, his landlady was laying face down on the kitchen floor, blood pouring from a shotgun wound to the head. Panic-stricken, he dashed frantically from house to house looking for help from any male neighbour, but Messrs Battin, Ades, Catt and Beaney were all at work and he could not inflict such a ghastly sight on their wives. Mrs Beaney saw Stone 'crying and wringing his hands ... in a dreadful state of agony'. He blurted out to Caroline Ades,[1] the blacksmith's wife, 'I've shot my mistress, I've shot her!' Tom Newman, a fellow navvy, saw Stone 'crying and running about the road, seemingly in great distress'. Tom entered the cottage to find Ann with her brains blown out and yet still alive and groaning. He dared not move her, but had absolutely no idea what to do.

Ann Beaney sent her young sons to fetch their father home from his workplace, Amoore's mill. When Sam Beaney arrived he found Stone in deep shock, with Tom Newman's arms 'clasped around him'. He sent a messenger to surgeon Frederick Ticehurst at 41 High Street. When carpenter John Battin arrived home he ran all the way to the gas works in Hastings town centre, where he broke the tragic news to George Harman and fetched him home. Poor Harman could not bear to look at his wife but sat sobbing in a neighbour's house.

When Mr Ticehurst arrived at 9pm Ann was dead.

The inquest was held on 24th October at the King's Head by Coroner Kell. George Stone swore he had 'never been in the habit of touching the gun, and did not know it stood loaded'. He merely lifted it and the chair knob caught the trigger.

Mr Ticehurst deposed that he found 'a large quantity of blood and brains' on the floor and ceiling of the wash-house, and 'picked up some pieces of her skull.' He found George Stone in the blacksmith's house, crying and shaking. Mr Ticehurst opined that 'It was quite evident' from Stone's demeanour that 'his share in the occurrence was involuntary'. Based on his and the neighbours' descriptions of Stone's intense distress and remorseful demeanour immediately after the incident, the jury's verdict was 'accidental death'.

In the 1851 census George Stone was lodging at Robertsbridge, along with many other navvies building the line from Tunbridge Wells to St Leonards. George Harman could not bear to stay in the cottage. He moved in with a workmate at 14 Stonefield Road, opposite the gas works. After he remarried he and his wife lived for many years at Gas Works Cottages. He died in 1896, long before his brother's grandson Arthur Harman lost his wife and then his life in tragic circumstances told in the story 'Indian Clubbing'.

References: *Sussex Advertiser* 25th September & 30th October 1849; *Daily News* 29th October 1849; *Evening Mail* 5th November 1849.

1. Caroline Ades began selling groceries and beer from their home. In the 1870s it became the Miller's Arms, with her son as licensee. The pub is still trading.

The newly-built sewage works in 1870.

The new town drainage system, started in 1856 and completed in 1868, included laying a major sewage pipe from the bottom of London Road, St Leonards, along the seafront to Rock-a-Nore. All the smaller sewers drained into it. The photo shows the inside of the main sewer pipe.

1870

THREE MEN DOWN

ROCK-A-NORE

By 1870 the 28,000 residents of Hastings were producing a million gallons of waste water and sewage every day. The Board of Health had lately installed a new sewer, 6ft high by 4ft wide, which was fed from smaller waste pipes, taking everything into an underground tank beneath the cliffs at Rock-a-Nore. The tank measured 200ft by 100ft and held 1.5m gallons. From it the sewage was taken through a half-mile iron outfall pipe and emptied into the sea at Ecclesbourne, where it became 'an inseparable and an indistinguishable part of the ocean'.

W.C. and R.G. Sillar were inspired by a Biblical passage which advocated 'sprinkling the unclean' with 'the blood of bulls and goats, and the ashes of an heifer'. They joined up with analytical chemist George Wigner and, by experimenting with **a**lum, **b**lood and **c**lay, invented the 'A.B.C. process' of converting human excrement into agricultural fertiliser. They patented it and in 1869 set up the Native Guano Company (NGC) in order to sell their 'novel and ingenious discovery' to councils and boards of health across Britain.

Meanwhile in Hastings, James Rock[1] pondered how best to deal with the town's sewage: there must be a better way than discharging human sewage into the sea, where people swam and fished, especially as each year saw an increase in residents and holiday makers. He read about the A.B.C. process, and in March 1870 he and 'a number of public spirited gentlemen' founded the Hastings Sewage Manure Company (HSMC) to introduce the process here.

The Board of Health provided the land and granted the NGC access to its giant tank at Rock-a-Nore on a 21-year lease at just £1 a year, and by June 1870 new works had been designed by William Andrews, the borough surveyor. A huge building was constructed above the spot where the sewer pipe discharged into the tank. Measuring 64 feet by 34 feet, it was made of red, yellow and black bricks and its sides were pierced with two rows of windows. The result was a 'handsome and spacious' edifice which had 'some pretensions to architectural beauty'. Internally it was 'admirably fitted up with first-class machinery ... tubes, tanks, and novel contrivances'. On the west side, hard against the cliff face, was a 60ft tall brick chimney. The works cost £4,200 (nearly half a million today).

1. James Rock (1819–1897) served as a councillor, alderman, mayor and chief magistrate as well as being involved in societies for archaeology, meteorology and philosophy, working men's clubs, mechanics' institutes and the Cinque Port Rifle Volunteer Corps. He was a designer and inventor, and had inherited from his father a prestigious carriage-building factory at 6 Stratford Place (now White Rock) which won a Gold Medal at the 1851 Great Exhibition. He lived at Fairlight, then 40 Magdalen Rd and later at Northiam.

The A.B.C. process separated the solid from the liquid, and then treated both in different ways. The liquid, once rendered 'clear and inodorous', could be discharged into shallow water, making lengthy outfall pipes redundant. The solids were purified, then agitated: 'Each tank has a revolving stirrer, propelled by a steam engine and consisting of twelve blades arranged spirally around a spindle. The mixture is then drawn up by means of an endless chain of buckets.' Once dried, the human manure was packed into sacks and offered for sale at £5 a hundredweight, and there was 'every promise of a brisk demand'.

In June a grand ceremonial inspection was attended by a host of civic dignitaries, many from far-off towns. At a sumptuous celebratory luncheon at the Queen's Hotel, speeches were given and toasts raised to the Native Guano Company. A jubilant James Rock happily accepted the credit and footed the bill. He asserted, with some pride, that the sewage of Hastings residents, 'instead of being wasted, was being utilised'. The mayor replied that the town was 'very much indebted' to Mr Rock, who was 'entitled to all the benefits he could make of it'. Replying to a suggestion that St Leonards should follow suit, surgeon Mr J.C. Savery shuddered. The town could not accommodate a 'manure manufactory', he argued, without 'prejudicing its interests', as neither its genteel residents nor its distinguished visitors would want it in — or anywhere near — their back yards.[1]

The A.B.C. works at Hastings aroused curiosity across England, Europe and the USA, and officials and engineers began to visit with a view to adopting the process themselves. 'No method of dealing with sewage ever excited more wide-spread interest', remarked the *HSLO*. The 'admirable system' was eulogised as 'skilfully planned and well executed'; it 'gives off no offensive odours' and would not disgust the olfactory nerves.

By July the works were producing thirty-seven tons of profitable manure every week, with 'the demand quite equal to the supply'. By August it was starting to dawn on councillors that the NGC had pulled a fast one: it was on track to make over £2,000 a year from the bodily waste of the fine citizens of Hastings, yet the town would receive only the £1 yearly rent. The council realised its mistake and opened negotiations with the NGC by asking for 2s 6d for each ton sold.

On Friday 5th August the division on the north side of the gigantic sewage tank was nearly empty. At 9pm two workmen, Paul Fry and Will Beaney, told the clerk of works that they intended to sweep it out. They needed a third man, and he told them to take William Nash. All three men were young, fit and in 'high spirits, and without any thought of the dreadful fate that awaited two of them'.

1. Two years earlier John Charles Savery (1830–1874), a physician, had published 'The Hastings and St Leonards Pamphlet', which highlighted the towns' new drainage system, its water supply, health, death-rate, and climate. His father was in practice here for fifty years and appears briefly in the chapter 'The Family Poisoner'.

Beaney was twenty-three and worked for the NGC. Fry, thirty-one, was nicknamed 'Bristol' because of his 'foreign' accent (he was actually from Wiltshire). An employee of the Local Board of Health, he lived in a tied cottage adjacent to the works. It was not his job to enter the tank but only to attend to the penstocks. At thirty-six Nash was the eldest. Born in Hastings, the son of a revenue officer, he served in the navy as a stoker before returning to his home town, where he rented one of Willett's Cottages in Ore and obtained work as a labourer for the HSMC.

Fry was first down the ladder, followed by young Beaney and then Nash. Fry walked across some planks to the cliff side, lit his pipe and complained that his eyes were stinging. Suddenly he cried out for help and collapsed into the water. Beaney dragged him out and put him on a wall, but he was overcome by noxious fumes. Nash held on to Fry whilst Beaney went up for fresh air and assistance.

Beaney's shouts for help were heard by John Thomas Porter, the HSMC's chemist. A Lincolnshire man, he had arrived in Hastings just a few weeks earlier and was lodging with a family in The Croft. 'With undaunted courage and commendable feeling towards his fellow creatures', Porter descended into the tank, a lighted candle in his hand. Samuel 'Curley' Harris, a stoker, followed him down, but before Porter reached the last rung his candle went out, he fell and Curley lost sight of him. Labourer George Standen, who was thirty and lived at 24 Rock-a-Nore Road, 'exhibited considerable coolness and courage' whilst trying in vain to rescue his workmates. By chance, George Wigner, co-inventor of the A.B.C. process, was on site that night. He descended twice and the second time he came back up he collapsed with breathing difficulties.

As news of the emergency spread, Borough Surveyor Andrews, Police Superintendent Glenister and two medical men arrived, swiftly followed by a reporter from the HSLO, who later described 'the state of excitement and confusion into which all were thrown'. By then all the sewage works' staff had been overcome with fumes and forced to come up for air, dizzy and exhausted. Bystanders pitched in or ran to fetch help. Coastguardman John Brown was allowed by PC Noakes to descend with a rope around his waist, but was quickly hauled back up, half asphyxiated.

It was a group of weatherbeaten fishermen who finally effected the rescue. They went down and returned with two lifeless bodies, whose faces were so thickly covered with raw sewage that they had to be washed before their workmates recognised them as Paul Fry and William Nash. The doctors, Charles Ashenden and (the aforementioned) J.C. Savery, tried to resuscitate them, but it was too late. The bodies were carried to the Pierwarden's store at the foot of All Saints' Street, which acted as a makeshift mortuary. Rescuers searched fruitlessly for John Porter, and concluded that his body must have been washed out to sea through the outfall pipe.

An inquest into the 'melancholy disaster' was held the next day in the Auction Room of the Swan Hotel in the High Street, under coroner Frederick Ticehurst.[1] The jurymen viewed the bodies and visited the scene of the tragedy. Mr Ashenden explained that he had saturated a piece of paper with lead and placed it over the mouth of one of the deceased shortly after rescue. The experiment revealed the presence of sulpheretted hydrogen. Despite that, the jury's verdict was that all three men died 'by inhaling noxious gases but how those gases were generated there is no cause to show'.

Sulpheretted hydrogen (latterly called hydrogen sulfide) is created when raw sewage is stored for a long time in hot weather, such as in Hastings in August. As it ferments and putrefies, it produces a colourless chalcogen hydride gas with a distinctive, foul odour like rotten eggs. It is very poisonous, corrosive, and flammable, and is an asphyxiant that suffocates victims at the cellular level, rendering cells in the body unable to use oxygen. Its toxicity is comparable with that of carbon monoxide, and short-term, high-level exposure can induce immediate collapse, with loss of breathing and a high probability of death.

During the inquest a message had arrived to say that the body of the chemist, John Porter, had been found in the iron sewer pipe about eight hundred yards from the tank and hauled out through a manhole. Porter's death received the most attention. At twenty-three he was the youngest victim, and was described as 'a man of considerable intelligence ... at the outset of a career which was full of promise', who had 'nobly lost his life in an endeavour to save others'.

Shortly before the tragedy Hastings Council received a memorial signed by about 250 inhabitants complaining about a foul stench emanating from the sewage works. Councillor Poole remarked on the pervasiveness of the 'nauseous odour': 'Whenever the wind was south-west it could be perceived at the top of High Street, and with a south-east wind in Ecclesbourne Valley'. However, this was not why the NGC pulled out of Hastings in 1874. The company directors cited an insufficient return on their capital outlay. James Rock said he felt that the NGC had 'skinned' him and then used him as their fall guy.

In 1874 the 'handsome and spacious' building was converted into a disinfecting station for the workhouse, apart from one section, which was used as a mortuary (until a purpose-built one was constructed on the other side of Rock-a-Nore Road in 1876). The chimney was demolished around 1900 and the remainder of the site was cleared in the late 1940s. Some remnants of the 1870 brickwork remain. The Motor Boat and Yacht Club and its rear car park are situated where the building used to be, whilst the eastern side of Rock-a-Nore car park covers the site of the giant underground tank.

References: *Maidstone Telegraph* 9th July & 13th August 1870; *HSLO* 4th & 18th June & 13th August 1870; *Leamington Advertiser* 9th June 1870; *Standard* 8th August 1870; *Lincolnshire Chronicle* 19th August 1870; *Hampshire Advertiser* 1st June 1870.

1. Mr Ticehurst was prominent in the chapter 'The Family Poisoner'.

1877

LETHAL LINIMENT

ST MARGARET'S TERRACE

At 10.30pm on Thursday 21st December, newly qualified doctor Richard Heath, twenty-six, was summoned from his home and surgery at 16 Warrior Square to nearby 1 St Margaret's Terrace. In a set of rented rooms at the top of the house he met sisters Rosa, Emily and Alice Marsden, middle-class spinsters in their thirties. Rosa had been violently sick after taking an indigestion remedy and was writhing on a bed, her pupils wildly dilated and her extremities ice cold.

Dr Heath asked to examine the medicine bottle, and immediately realised that the contents did not match the label. He could smell belladonna, a deadly poison. Rosa had ingested four spoonfuls, amounting to two fluid ounces — enough to kill six people — but her copious vomiting had saved her life. He administered an emetic to expel any remaining in her system, and stayed at her side for several hours.

Rosa had taken ABC Liniment, a mixture of **a**conite, **b**elladonna and **c**hloroform, which had been prescribed for Alice's rheumatism. To prevent unintentional ingestion, liniment was always dispensed in bottles of green or blue glass which were fluted and embossed or labelled 'Poison: Not To Be Taken'. When Dr Heath asked why it was not in a fluted bottle, Alice initially claimed not to know, then admitted that, six months previously, a bottle of ABC had arrived with its neck damaged, so she poured the contents into an empty bottle of indigestion medicine, 'trusting to remember the change'.

During his rounds the next morning, Dr Heath found Rosa much improved. However, over the course of the day her nervous system and lungs failed and by midnight she was dead. She was only thirty-two.

An inquest opened at the Norman Hotel the next day. Coroner Charles Davenport Jones and the jury visited St Margaret's Terrace to view the body. Permission for burial was granted, and the inquest adjourned. Rosa was coffined but remained with her sisters until Boxing Day, when, after a modest service at St Mary Magdalen church, she was quietly buried in the Borough Cemetery.

At the resumed inquest a teenage errand boy admitted to dropping a liniment bottle en route to Alice at 17 Plynlimmon Terrace (their previous lodgings). He handed it to their landlady, Mrs Campany, and later mentioned the mishap to a colleague, who told James Bell, the pharmacist. When Alice did not return the bottle, Mr Bell thought nothing more of it.

Selina Campany confirmed that a liniment bottle arrived broken. Half its contents were missing, and Alice asked her to transfer what was left into a blue fluted bottle which had previously held mustard liniment. When the Marsdens

1 St Margaret's Terrace in 1905.

The Norman Hotel. It was rebuilt in the 1930s and is now the Piper public house.

moved out in October they had left it behind. The bottle was now in the hands of the police, who had shown it to James Bell. His super-sensitive olfactory nerve detected mustard liniment but no belladonna or aconite. He had also taken a good sniff of Rosa's 'indigestion remedy' and it reeked of belladonna.

Alice changed her story. Aware that whoever decanted the liniment into an unmarked bottle could be charged with manslaughter, she denied previously admitting it. She had no idea who the culprit was.

The coroner declared the evidence 'most unsatisfactory'. If whoever transferred the liniment did not warn others, it was manslaughter. If that person intended someone to drink it, then it was murder. Contradictory stories left the jury unable to return anything but an open verdict.

Rosa's death can only have been accidental if she failed to recognise the smell of belladonna, first when she opened the bottle, and then when she lifted each spoonful to her lips. The jury knew that she should have recognised the smell because she used liniment on Alice for her rheumatism, but they did not know the full story:

> Rosa Marsden and her sisters were infinitely more familiar with belladonna than ... almost anyone else in the country ... It had been the main agent in their father's first and much vaunted homeopathic cure ... in the 1840s, and he had been prescribing it in various forms ... ever since. On countless occasions his daughters would have collected supplies of the drug from [a chemist] and probably even helped their father prepare doses. Alice's regular treatment with ABC Liniment represented only a tiny percentage of their collective familiarity with the poison.[1]

If one or both sisters intended to kill Rosa by stealth, they would not use something she would recognise. With accident and murder ruled out, it had to be suicide, despite Rosa's accepting an emetic. People have been known to take deadly poison whilst in severe mental distress, then change their minds, make themselves sick and call for medical help.

Rosa died during a Christmas visit from her sister, which seems an unlikely time to commit suicide, but their past does shed light on her psyche, because in the 1850s the sisters had been central figures in an infamous child abuse scandal.

Their father, James Loftus Marsden, was a progressive and celebrated homeopathic physician who founded a grand water-cure establishment at Great Malvern. In private he was a selfish man who kept his wife in a state of near-perpetual pregnancy, then forced her to abandon their six young children because he demanded she attend to his needs during a prolonged visit to Egypt, Austria and Malta. The youngest, Rosa, was only two when they left, and Alice was born in Vienna during the trip. Two years later, in 1847, poor Mrs Marsden died in childbirth.

1. Pauline Conolly (2013) *The Water Doctor's Daughters*, p224.

The Marsden children had an unusual upbringing. Their father's spa was patronised by the rich and famous, and they met many eminent people, including Charles Dickens and Alfred, Lord Tennyson. But they lacked the secure, unconditional love of a mother and were raised by a series of hired servants. They gained their father's attention by taking an interest in his work and, when they were old enough, by assisting him.

In March 1852 Dr Marsden began romancing a new lady friend (they would marry at the end of that year). He sent his only son to boarding school, and placed his daughters in the care of a French governess, Célestine Doudet. Before long Doudet told Dr Marsden that all five girls, aged between six and thirteen, were addicted to 'self-abuse'. Utterly mortified, Marsden whipped Rosa, who was just eight, and instructed Doudet to cure the girls with physical restraints, a rigid homeopathic diet and any other means she saw fit.

When Doudet returned to Paris, Marsden asked her to take his girls with her. Once under her exclusive control she kept them in a state of continual mental and physical terror by introducing 'a system of heartless correction and of unheard-of chastisement'. She starved them, locked them in a cellar, dragged them around by the hair and flung them against walls. Afterwards she would inflict mental abuse by forcing them to write home singing the praises of their kind and loving governess.

One day Doudet battered twelve-year-old Marian so viciously that she went into a coma. Her subsequent death prompted Dr Marsden to visit. He found Lucy and Emily so emaciated that he barely recognised them, whilst Alice and Rosa were in a bed together, their ankles tied to the footboard. Rosa was 'black and scarred from head to foot'. The girls were brought home immediately but Lucy died of an illness soon afterwards, 'enfeebled by malnutrition'.

In 1855 Doudet was tried for the murder of Marian but was acquitted. A second trial found her guilty of child cruelty and she was sentenced to five years in prison. Emily, Rosa and Alice were taken back to Paris to give evidence at the trials, which were covered extensively by the English and French press.[1] No thought was given to their mental wellbeing and their identities were not protected but widely published, together with salacious details of their abuse, and degrading lies about 'phrenzied' masturbation. The judge feared that the slur had 'sullied their honour and future prospects'.

The three girls were left deeply traumatised, both by the long-term abuse and by the ordeal of the trials. The physical wounds healed, but they were emotionally scarred. They constantly changed lodgings, moving between various spa towns and seaside resorts, never able to settle. The two youngest, Alice and Rosa, became increasingly neurotic and obsessed with their health: Rosa's dressing table was 'cluttered with medicine bottles' and, whilst packing to move (yet again) they gathered up another thirty or so.

1. In 1956 the story of Célestine Doudet's abuse of the Marsden children was the subject of *Le Procès de Célestine Doudet ou le Secret de Mademoiselle,* an episode in a French docu-drama series called 'En votre âme et conscience' ('In your soul and conscience').

None of the three sisters married or had romances. Distrustful of others, they lived in close confinement with one another, with little social life beyond church. They clung to each other for company: an undiluted, ever-present reminder of their past. Such a hothouse atmosphere could magnify feelings of guilt, jealousy, recrimination, bitterness and resentment left over from the trauma of their formative years, and it seems they somehow led to Rosa's death, probably by her own hand.

Epilogue: Dr Marsden and Hastings

Dr Marsden's second marriage was very happy and lasted twenty-four years. In 1876, the year before Rosa died, the elderly Marsden ran off with a servant girl forty years his junior. His daughters were shocked at his bringing further scandal on their family name by his shameless adultery and wicked fornication. They were especially appalled by his cruelty to his devoted wife, who did not deserve to be humiliated and deserted in her old age. All three of his daughters disowned him and, to show solidarity and compassion, Emily moved in with his abandoned wife. The following year she travelled to St Leonards to spend Christmas with her sisters, and a few days later Rosa was dead.

Ten years after Rosa died and Alice and Emily had left Sussex forever, Dr Marsden moved, with his young mistress and their child, to 17 Ashburnham Road. This was odd because neither had any previous connection to Hastings. When Marsden died in 1891 it was revealed that he had made arrangements to be interred in Rosa's grave in the Borough Cemetery, suggesting perhaps his reason for moving here as he approached the end of his life.

References: *London Daily News* 13th December 1854, 12th February, 1st & 12th March 1855; *HSLO* 29th December 1877.

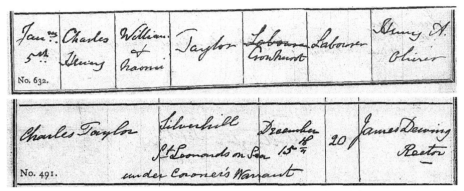

Documents of a life cut short. The baptism (5th January 1862) and burial (15th December 1881) records for Charles Henry Taylor, from the parish register of the church of St George, Crowhurst.

Looking west towards Silverhill junction in 1905. The shops on the left were built onto the front of Lorne Villas. Grove Cottages ran parallel to and behind them, in Grove Road (now Strood Road).

1881

(Un)natural Death

Silverhill

In May 1878 Battle Petty Sessions granted a bastardy order to eighteen-year-old Emily Eldridge of Baldslow. Charles Henry Taylor, seventeen, was ordered to pay her 2s a week to help support their two-month-old son.[1] Charles told the magistrates they would marry when he could afford it. Three years later, in July 1881, they married and Charles moved in with Emily's parents and her six siblings at 2 Grove Cottages, Silverhill. This increased to eleven the number living in the modest, four-roomed dwelling. Emily worked in Mrs Lucas's laundry, next door at no.3, whilst Charles was a farm labourer.

When he arrived home from work on Friday 9th December, Charles ate a meal prepared by his wife, which included some slices of a cake she had baked. Soon afterwards he was stricken with severe vomiting and purging, which continued for thirty-six miserable hours. Emily put him to bed, where he remained under her constant wifely care. The next day he spat out some bread and butter she served him, but gratefully accepted tea and water to quench his huge thirst. The liquids she gave him also made him vomit and purge, and he developed a terrible headache. He alternated between sweats and chills and at times shivered so violently that the iron bedstead rattled.

It was not until 11.15pm the following day that Emily asked her mother to walk the dozen yards to 1 Lorne Villas and fetch Dr Thomas Prickard Harvey. He refused to attend because the family were not patients of his. Mrs Eldridge did not try another doctor, although there was one in nearby Springfield Road.

Throughout the night Charles continued to vomit and purge, and became delirious and hallucinated. 'He kept pulling at the blanket,' Emily explained. She asked him to stop, but he replied: 'I can't help it'. She said that at 4.15am he 'threw his hands about as though he was convulsed', then fell quiet. Emily's brother John thought him 'either dead or gone in a fit', and at 5am he called at Dr Harvey's. This time he agreed to attend. Arriving minutes later he found Charles already cold and stiff, signifying that he had been dead for hours.

On 15th December, eleven days short of his twenty-first birthday, Charles was interred at Crowhurst, the place he was born and where his grieving family still lived.

The inquest began the next day. It was held by Charles Sheppard and took three sessions to complete. In an *ad hoc* courtroom within the Clarence

---

1. The boy was baptised not at their local church but at St Mary-in-the-Castle in Pelham Crescent. According to the parish register, Emily's parents pretended the child was theirs.

The Clarence Hotel, on the corner of Beaufort Road.

Hotel, Emily recounted the gruesome details of her young husband's demise. She was keen to point out that on Friday she, Charles and their three-year-old son had all eaten the same food. Perhaps she believed this proved he was not poisoned; in fact it did the opposite — it eliminated rancid food as the cause.

Dr Harvey described the contents of Charles's chamber pot as 'blackish green' and revealed that the post mortem showed that his stomach was 'coated with a yellowish slime' which had 'numbers of minute white particles' mixed up in it. He concluded that death was due to 'the administration of an irritant'. This was a sensational finding because it hinted at murder.

Knowing that Dr Harvey, as an ordinary family GP, had little or no training or experience in forensics or poisoning, the coroner asked others to help him find out exactly what the mysterious white particles were. Dr Hubert Hudson, a GP at Battle, and chemist Horace Fabian Cheshire, the public analyst for Hastings Council, were assigned to assist. A portion of Charles's stomach was sent to Home Office analyst Dr Thomas Stevenson at Guy's Hospital in London.

The inquest was adjourned to await toxicology reports. Gossips expected them to prove foul play. Why else were experts poring over Charles's viscera? He was a fit, strong youth of twenty who was engaged daily in arduous physical work; moreover, he was described as being 'in perfect health'. It would take a lot more than a bout of food poisoning to kill such a man.

At the resumed inquest Dr Hudson, Mr Cheshire and Dr Stevenson reported that they concurred with Dr Harvey: death was caused by an irritant; however, they did not know what it was and could find no trace of poison. The coroner suggested that the cause of death was 'inflammation of the bowels', but the jury chose instead 'death from natural causes'. Because of this verdict, the police had no powers to investigate.

If the cause of Charles's death were indeed natural, then a likely culprit was viral gastroenteritis ('stomach flu') and severe dehydration resulting from thirty-six hours of vomiting and purging whilst taking in insufficient fluids. However, this does not account for the confusion, delirium, convulsions and seizures which Charles experienced in the hour before he expired.

Although the jury inexplicably ignored it, the analysis of Charles's internal organs showed that he had ingested an irritant. His symptoms — vomiting, purging, sweating, hallucinations, confusion, delirium, convulsions and seizures — matched exactly those of acute arsenical poisoning. He even 'kept pulling at the blanket', just like Flaubert's Madame Bovary, whose hands 'plucked at her bedsheets' as she writhed in the agony of suicide by arsenic.

Arsenic trioxide, known as white arsenic, was virtually undetectable when slipped into foodstuffs and drinks. In the Victorian era it was known as 'the poisoner's substance of choice', and from 1750 to 1914 it featured in 237 cases to come before the English courts.

The Sale of Arsenic Regulation Act 1851 required purchasers to sign a register; however, arsenic was also used commercially and was commonly mixed with soft-soap to destroy bedbugs. Emily worked in a commercial laundry, which probably kept it on the premises.

Charles's symptoms matched arsenic poisoning and Emily could have obtained it. However, no trace of it — nor of any other poison — was found by two GPs and two public analysts, one of whom, Dr Stevenson, was Britain's leading toxicologist and an expert witness in many notable trials, who would be knighted by Edward VII in 1904 for his services to public health. It seems impossible that this team could have made a mistake, overlooked something, or failed to test for every possible poison.

The Charles Taylor case is truly a conundrum that will never be solved.

Epilogue: the fate of Emily and William

After 1881, Emily appears in few available documents and always as 'Emma'. From 1887 to 1901 she was summoned and fined a dozen times for failing to send her son to school regularly. In the 1901 census she was working as an ironer in a laundry and lodging at 19 Wellington Terrace (now Duke Road). Though Charles had been dead for nearly twenty years, she had not remarried, but lived with her son, then twenty-three, who was an unskilled labourer.

References: *Lincolnshire Chronicle* 22nd August 1862; *HSLO* 17th, 24th and 31st December 1881 & various 1887–1891.

Arthur Holman was short in stature and had dark brown hair, dark brown eyes, a swarthy complexion and a cross anchor and heart tattooed on his left arm. Image: naval records, c1918.

1889

THE KILLER SPOKE

MARKET PASSAGE

Opposite 18 South Street there used to be an archway leading to a dismal, cobbled courtyard just 15ft square, around which ten workers' cottages were built in the 1840s. There were five on either side and each contained two rooms measuring 12ft by 8ft, one above the other, linked by a steep, narrow wooden staircase. In the lower room a modest coal fire was provided, which did double duty as both a heater and a cooker. The only sanitation was a well and four privies in the courtyard, shared by all the residents of the ten cottages, their visitors and the odd passer-by caught short.

Despite its glamorous name Crystal Square was, by all accounts, a slum. As early as 1855 the town clerk had described its children as 'swarming with vermin', whilst some of its houses were already 'in a disgraceful state' of disrepair. However, a shortage of cheap accommodation ensured that the square was always fully occupied. In 1861 nine of the tiny dwellings housed five or more people and one was home to eleven. There were frequent squabbles, drunken quarrels and the occasional fist-fight, but the residents were hardworking people, including bricklayers, laundresses, stone masons, dressmakers, house painters, chimney sweeps and labourers.

Many children were born and raised in the square and grew up together, neighbours and siblings alike. In 1881 no.15 (on the north side) was home to fly driver William Reynolds, his girlfriend Mary Leach and their five children. Two doors away at no.13 were William and Susan Holman. They had lived in the square for at least ten years and their three children had been born there. The youngest, aged four, had been christened with the grand name of Arthur Charles Augustus Gibbs Holman.

By 1889 William and Mary had been married for five years and had added three more children to their brood. Their son Billy, fifteen, had been working for Marchant's perambulator and cycle manufactory for three years. Although Arthur Holman was only twelve, he had already been hired and fired by Thomas Marchant and had been taken on as an errand boy for another firm.

On 24th October Arthur entered Marchant's shop at 17 London Road and began pelting Billy Reynolds with beans until he got cross and threatened to thrash him. Later, when Billy was at the cycle depot in Market Passage, off Norman Road, Arthur showed up again. Angry words were exchanged and Arthur grabbed a heavy steel spoke used for tricycle wheels and hurled it at Billy with all his might. It hit the back of his head, drawing blood. Billy shouted, 'You have split my head open!' Arthur retorted, 'Serves you right', and ran away.

Billy realised that the spoke was actually embedded in his head and, worse, he could not pull it out. The owner's son, Tommy Marchant, was obliged to use some force to extract it. Concerned about the open hole in Billy's skull, he took the boy to Dr Joseph at 11 Grand Parade, who dressed the wound and advised Billy to go home and rest. Two days later the lad became insensible, and despite being admitted to hospital and undergoing an operation, he died at 2am on Sunday 27th October. The post mortem, performed by Dr A.R. Ticehurst,[1] revealed that the spoke had caused a puncture fracture of the skull, penetrating it to the astonishing depth of three-and-a-half-inches. The police were informed and Sergeant Love was despatched to Crystal Square, where he found Arthur and arrested him.

The inquest jury returned a verdict of manslaughter, and Arthur's father and two family friends stood sureties of £25 each to ensure he would turn up for the hearing at the police court. On the day of the hearing, the court was packed with excited spectators eager to catch a glimpse of the boy killer. Arthur, who 'appeared keenly touched by his position', broke down in sobs. Magistrate Henry Winter remarked that he 'regretted exceedingly' having to commit such a young boy to the Winter Assizes, but he was duty-bound to do so.[2]

When Arthur stood trial at County Hall in Lewes he was two weeks short of his thirteenth birthday. The prosecutor, Marshall Hall, was a bright young barrister en route to a knighthood, as was the defence counsel, C.F. Gill.[3] Gill argued that there was insufficient evidence, and quoted Blackstone's ruling that a child under fourteen was *doli incapax* unless evidence of malice was proven. Mr Justice Denman pointed out that it was indeed proven: 'Far from being sorry and apologising', Arthur 'had used the revengeful expression that it served the other boy right'. However, he did not think the jury would care to convict a boy of such tender years on the flimsy evidence before them. The jury duly returned a unanimous verdict of 'not guilty'.

By 1891 the Holmans had moved two doors along to no.11 Crystal Square, putting a little more distance between themselves and the Reynolds family. Arthur was absent, but reappears in records in June 1892, when, aged fifteen, he enlisted in the navy. As an able seaman he served his country for thirty-seven years, and during the First World War he was a gunner on a battleship. In this fashion, Arthur paid his debt to society in a far better way than spending years in prison.

A 1937 council report labelled Crystal Square as 'unfit for human habitation' and scheduled it for compulsory purchase and clearance. When the Second World War started there were still fifteen residents, but Crystal Square's days were numbered. The site is now covered by Crystal Square Car Park.

---

1. Augustus Rowland Ticehurst, son of Frederick, who features in several other chapters.
2. Henry Winter JP (1817–1900), was Mayor of Hastings in 1880, and his name can still be seen today, etched into a corner stone of Hastings Town Hall.
3 Later Sir Edward Marshall Hall KC, MP (1858–1927), known as 'the Great Defender'; later Sir Charles Frederick Gill KC (1851–1923) Director of Public Prosecutions.

1891

TRAIN TRACK TRAGEDY

BOPEEP TUNNEL

Tuesday 25th August started out as just another working day for Edgar Dunk, a fifty-six-year-old platelayer[1] on the South Eastern Railway. At 6.20am he was ambling eastwards through the 1,318-yard Bopeep Tunnel, checking the track was in good order. By the glimmer of his flickering paraffin lantern, he noticed something between the rails ahead. As he approached he realised it was a woman, laying face down, her head towards Warrior Square station, which was ninety yards away. She was motionless and not breathing, and there was a lot of blood on the track near her head.

Dunk walked on to the station and fetched Porter Titchener and two other workmates. Deep within the silent, dank tunnel they examined the scene by the light of four lanterns. There was no sign that the woman had crawled or been dragged, nor were her clothes bunched up or disarranged. One arm was beneath her, the other was straight out in front. A white straw hat lay a few yards away, one long hatpin through it, another pin was found close by.

Dealing with fatalities was a horrible but unavoidable duty for railway servants, but this one caused far more shock and upset because it was a young female. Everyone killed in Bopeep Tunnel since it was built had been a man doing his job; indeed, just five months earlier Titchener had helped carry a dead guard — and his severed leg — out of the same tunnel.[2] The railwaymen carried the woman to the porters' room on a board and placed her face upwards on the table. One of them knew her, but the swelling to her face and the black soot that covered her features rendered her unrecognisable.

A porter was despatched to fetch the nearest doctor, Henry Colborne, who lived nearby at 121 London Road. He guessed the age of the deceased as twenty-two or -three; but the girl's well nourished, mature body had deceived him. In fact the girl was nine days younger than his own daughter: both were thirteen and nine months. Her face was filthy and, as he picked off the bits of ballast and cleansed the dirt from her face, she began to appear younger.

PC Caleb King searched the girl for a clue to her identity, but her pockets held only handkerchiefs, gloves, a penny and a silver brooch. As word got about during the morning, people began to visit to see if they knew her. Eventually a teenage fly driver claimed she was his sister, Polly, then left to fetch his father.

---

1. A platelayer inspected and carried out minor repairs to the track on a day-to-day basis.
2. Ten people died in the tunnel between 1849 and 1928. All but this one were railwaymen.

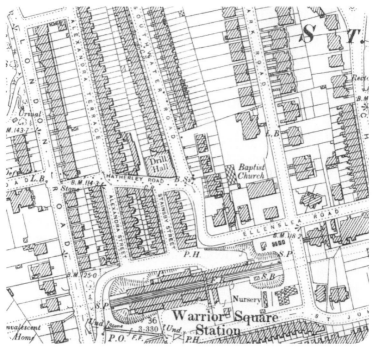

Alexandra Terrace (now Alexandra Road), Railway Cottages (opposite the drill hall), Ellenslea Road and Warrior Square station.

19 Alexandra Road in 2015.

Hearing her name, Joe Titchener returned to the porters' room. With her face clean and no longer swollen, he realised the girl was Polly Sheather, whose family lived a minute from his and a hundred yards from the station. He had known her since she was a baby, and his wife was her music teacher for three years. Polly was 'a cheerful girl, always full of play', and she would always stop and chat if she saw him on the station.

Thomas Sheather arrived and informed PC King that the girl was his youngest child, Agnes Mary, known as Polly. In 1856 Thomas, a Catsfield man, had married Agnes Hawkins, the daughter of the village shoemaker at Guestling Green.[1] He set up a business as a fly proprietor at Park House Mews, Ellenslea Road, where they lived above the stables and coachhouse where he kept his horses, carriages and bath chairs. Polly, their tenth and last child, was born in the mews on 25th October 1877.

Agnes died when Polly was nine and, just four months later, on 3rd January 1888, Thomas married Elizabeth Cornell. She was fourteen years his junior, and harboured a dark and guilty secret: she had left her husband and three children in east London and wed Thomas in her maiden name. The marriage was bigamous, illegal and invalid. We do not know the date she left her family, but when she met Thomas her son was thirteen and her twin daughters just six.[2] By 1891 Thomas had separated home and work, keeping the mews for business and moving his family into a modern home at 19 Alexandra Terrace. His elder children had flown, leaving only James, seventeen, and Polly, thirteen.

When Thomas last saw Polly at 6pm the evening before her death, she had been in a 'merry mood'. Six days previously she had started a new job as a domestic servant in a lodging house at 79 Warrior Square.[3] Her employer, Charles Cotton, was a married man of thirty-one who hailed from Brooklyn.[4] Polly lived in but visited her family every day. She told Cotton that she preferred living at his house because her father 'bullied' her and her stepmother was 'always drunk'. However, days later she told her parents that the job was too arduous and Mr Cotton was dissatisfied with her work.

On Monday 24th August, the day before Polly died, Mrs Sheather gave Mr Cotton five days' notice; however, Polly later told him that she did not want to resign. He passed this on to Mrs Sheather, adding that he wished her to stay. She told him that Polly told her that he often came home drunk and ill-treated her, his wife and a little boy in their care. Cotton was deeply affronted: 'For the

1. She grew up opposite the Geerings; see 'The Family Poisoner'.
2. Baker's daughter Elizabeth Cornell of Whitechapel, born 20th March 1848, married lead glazier William Fisher on 21st June 1868. By 1870 they were in the USA, where their son Herbert was born in 1874. They returned to London, where their twin daughters were born in 1881. William and his daughters appear in the 1891 census living in Hackney. He gave his status as 'widower'. By 1901 he, too, had remarried bigamously.
3. No.79 was destroyed by a bomb during WW2. A pumping station now covers the site.
4. Americans were rare in Hastings and St Leonards: only 0.5% of the 60,000 enumerated in the 1891 census had been born there.

reputation of my own house and character,' he declared, 'I cannot allow such scandal to go on. I must ask her what it means, and bring her before you and her father tomorrow morning'.

Back at home he dared Polly to repeat her slurs to his face. She accused her stepmother of being a 'wicked, base woman' who had made it up. Mr Cotton declared himself weary of her 'bringing tales backwards and forwards'. Instead of working till Saturday, Polly offered to go home immediately, but he declined. About 10.15pm she wished him and his wife goodnight as usual and left to go up to bed. Ten minutes later he found the front door wide open and Polly missing. He went out for an hour, visiting the Railway Inn, opposite Warrior Square station, and then the Yorkshire Grey, near the foot of London Road.

Mr Cotton had a side-job collecting payment for coal supplied to local households. The next morning, whilst going from door to door, he heard talk about a girl killed on the railway line. Calling on Mrs Sheather he handed over Polly's wages and as they chatted it emerged that she had not been home. He shared the news, fearing it was Polly. Mrs Sheather suggested he tell her husband, who was at the seafront cab rank. Crossing the lattice footbridge Mr Cotton met telegraph clerk Alfred Kennett, son of the station master. His description of the deceased matched Polly, so Cotton returned to Mrs Sheather and shared his fears. He recalled her response as: 'Oh the wicked girl, she said she would do it' but her neighbour later claimed it was: 'No, no, it cannot be her!'

An inquest was held by Charles Davenport Jones over three evenings: 26th August at the Market Hall in George Street, and 2nd and 7th September at Hastings Town Hall. During the first session the jury walked to Rock-a-Nore mortuary. Polly was formally identified and an order given for burial. On 29th August she was interred in the churchyard of St Laurence, Catsfield.

News of the tragedy having appeared in the press, the second and third inquest sessions were crowded to capacity. The gossips wondered why the Sheather family had engaged a solicitor.[1] Depositions were taken from family, friends and railwaymen. When Dr Colborne took the stand the court was 'cleared of all females and children', in case anything of a sexual nature was mentioned. The doctor found no evidence that she had been 'outraged' (raped). However, when he remarked that, 'In the strict sense, she was not *virgo intacta*', those present probably leapt to the erroneous conclusion that this proved she had 'been with a man', a shocking notion, given her age.

Dr Colborne's report came as a surprise to those who assumed Polly had been run over by a train. He explained that she had died from a small, triangular shaped skull fracture behind her right ear, caused by a single, powerful blow from something like a wrench hammer, crowbar, jemmy or other heavy iron implement with a sharp right angle.

1. He was a newly-qualified twenty-eight-year-old called Frederick George Langham (1863-1946), and he was the grandson of John Pearson's solicitor J.G. Langham (see 'The Cook of Caterina Villa').

Tools like that were used to repair the track, but police searches had found nothing in the tunnel, nor on the embankments, related to Polly's death. On the track where her body had lain there was a lot of blood, including one streak three feet long. The doctor thought Polly might have been killed by an engine if it had something on the front capable of causing her head injury, although if she had been pitched violently face-first onto sharp ballast and rough-hewn timber sleepers, her face would have sustained extensive cuts and bruises. As it was, there was only one small mark on her forehead, which had not even broken the skin.

Having examined Polly at 6.50am, and watched rigor mortis develop over the course of the day, Colborne put the time of death at between 2am and 3am. No train ran between the 12.10am mail and a light engine at 5.45am; however, according to research published in 2009, Polly could have died as early as 11pm or as late as 5am:

> Despite attempts over a hundred years to develop methods for precise estimation of the time of death, the accuracy of these methods ... still leaves a margin for improvement. During the first 6h after death, there is at least a 2h margin of error, but in the next 14h, the margin of error increases to at least 3h.

When Joe Titchener took the stand it was clear that he was under suspicion. He admitted that Polly 'was in the habit of running up to me, or calling out when she saw me on the platform'. In the week before her death she had crossed the footbridge twice a day, yet he claimed not to have seen her. It was also odd that he said he did not recognise her when he recovered her body, nor when she lay face upwards on a table in daylight.[1]

Station staff were quizzed about Joe's movements the night before Polly was found. Apart from going home for supper at 10pm for half an hour, he was on the station from 6pm until 11.15pm. After that only he and the signalman remained. Bopeep Tunnel and the signalbox were at opposite ends of the station, and after the gas lamps were turned off at 11.15pm the Bopeep end was too dark to be seen from the box. The signalman left about 1am, and from then until 5.30am (when a new signalman came on duty) Joe was alone.

The coroner remarked upon Polly's attachment to the station, calling it 'a peculiar place' for a girl to visit. A young laundress revealed that she and Polly would hang about the station, often till late at night, 'passing remarks on people'. Other girls said Polly was miserable because her stepmother ill-treated her and called her an 'overgrown lout'. Her father gave his wife 1s 6d a week towards clothing her, but instead she spent it on beer. Polly wanted to become a live-in domestic servant, just to get away from her.

1. Joe lived for twenty years at 4 Railway Cottages (renumbered 15 Southwater Rd) eight dwellings built by the railway company to house staff. Joe died from pneumonia in 1896, aged forty-three.

Warrior Square station, looking west towards the mouth of Bopeep Tunnel.

Staff at Warrior Square c1890. They are on the up side, with Bopeep Tunnel behind them. Station master Kennett is seated in the centre and Porter Titchener is standing, on the far left. The others are porters, booking office staff, a ticket collector, a signalman and his box-boy. The man in 'civvies' is probably the goods agent.

After twenty-five years as station master at Hastings Bishop Kennett (1819–1894) was transferred to Warrior Square, where he lived with his family in the flat above the offices. He died there, having completed fifty-two years in railway service. Three years after Polly's death, Elizabeth and Caroline Sheather (Polly's elder sister) attended his funeral, whilst Porter Titchener was a pallbearer (and died just two years later).

Under the coroner's direction, the jury returned an open verdict. This caused controversy, and 'a large crowd assembled in the vicinity of the Town Hall and remained till a late hour discussing with keen interest the result of the enquiry and the failure to elucidate the mystery'. Some locals hinted that Joe Titchener had something to do with Polly's death; others whispered that the stepmother's cruelty drove her to kill herself. In her own defence, Mrs Sheather wrote a letter, which was published in the *HSLO*.

> Sir, —I think it my duty to clear my character of the imputations cast upon it at the inquest on my stepdaughter ... On Monday last several witnesses (young girls) were brought up to speak against me, who had not the slightest knowledge of either myself or her home. In fact, I had no idea she had any acquaintance with such girls. The deceased had a good and comfortable home, which I should be pleased to show to anyone, a kind and indulgent father, and, with regard to myself, I have a clear conscience that I did my duty by her to the best of my ability. She required a kind and firm hand, but like many other girls of her age, did not like correction although it was for her own good. ... [Polly] was a particularly bright and happy girl, and whatever has been said she was most loving and affectionate towards me, and the last girl in the world to commit suicide. I can stand before God with a clear conscience, knowing that I did my best in every way for her.

The level of literacy and phrasing strongly suggests that the letter was written not by Mrs Sheather but by her Cambridge-educated solicitor. Her dissatisfaction with the verdict was shared by many locals, some boldly asserting that it should have been 'wilful murder'. The editor of the *HSLO* admitted that certain 'suspicious elements ... pointed towards' murder, and he felt sure that 'the police will not fail to make the needful discoveries' because they were 'prosecuting investigations anew in the hope of ascertaining whether the unhappy girl came to her end by foul means'. However, the case was never again mentioned in the press.

Accident, suicide, murder?

If Polly's death was suicide or an accident, she first needed to enter the tunnel unobserved.[1] According to railwaymen, no girl could climb over the tall iron railings, but there was another way: she could have entered the station before the gates were locked and hid in the female toilets until everyone but Joe had gone. Railwaymen never entered them, not even for cleaning, because the ladies' room attendant did it during her daytime shift. Polly could have waited until Titchener was busy then slipped along the platform and into the tunnel.

1. Entering the tunnel from the other end would entail walking one-and-a-half miles by road and avoiding detection by several staff, because there were two stations, sidings, and a raised signalbox which had a clear view of the tunnel mouth and all the tracks and walkways leading to it.

Another route to Bopeep Tunnel: the red-brick curved wall on the left could hide someone coming down the embankment from Joe Titchener's view.

Bopeep Tunnel had a single track through the centre, leaving plenty of space each side to pass through it in perfect safety.[1] If Polly was killed by accident she must have been walking unnecessarily close to the track. Steam engines are noisy, but if one were coasting at low speed, without its whistle being blown on entering the tunnel, Polly could have been caught unawares.

If Polly had killed herself, then her method was both unique and bizarre. Railway suicides were described (in gory detail) in the press: people either laid across a track, placed their neck on a rail, or jumped in front of a train. Polly must have stood or walked alongside the track and been struck a glancing blow from a passing train.

We know that Polly walked alongside the track and not between the rails, because nothing on the front of an engine could have caused the triangular shaped skull fracture she sustained. Had she stood between the rails and been stuck from behind, her head, neck or shoulder would have been bashed in by a heavy iron coupling or a buffer, both of which were smooth. Engines and carriages did have fittings that matched her injury: the outside corners of the engine frame, iron-edged footboards, external steps and lamp brackets. However, these protruded from the sides or the outside front corners, not the centre-front between the wheels. Therefore, to have been hit by something which could inflict the triangular skull fracture, Polly must have been walking or standing alongside the rails.

What is more, she must have remained on her feet whilst the train passed, then stepped over a rail before falling forwards onto her face between the rails. This is impossible, because such a blow would have pitched her violently to the ground and the injury would have caused instant death.

1. The tunnel was built wide enough to accommodate two tracks, but between 1885 and 1906 only one central track was used. This was due to problems with defective brickwork.

Josephine and Joseph Titchener.
Studio portrait c1895 by D.J. Eddy
of 41 Norman Road.

Polly Sheather, from the *HSLO*.

AGNES MARY SHEATHER.

Only one solution fits the forensic evidence: Polly was murdered.

Dr Colborne's assessment, based on his post mortem, was that Polly's injuries were caused by a heavy tool. The assailant must have placed her in the tunnel in the hope that the head injury matched being hit by a train. The careful placement of her hat and its pin neatly on the track could have been the killer's attempt to make it look like suicide. Suspicion had fallen on Joe Titchener solely because he knew Polly and was alone on the station when she died. But he had no reason to harm her. Mr Cotton was peeved with Polly for lying about him, and he did go out for an hour right after she left. But he, too, had no motive to inflict a brutal attack.

Elizabeth Sheather had ample motive: three years of being increasingly wound up by her difficult, tale-telling stepchild. She had abandoned her own little girls before they were six, suggesting a lack of maternal feeling even towards her own flesh and blood. In her letter she admitted to using 'a firm hand' and 'correction' — euphemisms for beating children when they 'needed' it. If Polly went home and told her stepmother that she had walked out of her job, and Mrs Sheather were drunk, she may have lost her temper and thwacked Polly with any random implement that happened to be close to hand. However, she could not have carried Polly's body from the house, through the streets, over the fence, down the embankment and into the tunnel. If she killed Polly then it must have been Thomas who disposed of the body in order to save his wife from the gallows. Alternatively, maybe he killed Polly.

It may seem unlikely that a father could murder his own daughter, but a search of newspapers during that era unearthed twenty such cases, of which two involved a teenager. In 1895 Thomas Brooks killed his fourteen-year-old daughter by cutting her throat at a station in Manchester, and in 1905 William Hancocks stabbed his fifteen-year-old, for which he was hanged for murder.

One route to Bopeep Tunnel: the alley leading from the forecourt to the up side platform close to the tunnel mouth. Above: a landau cab.

Perhaps when Polly left Mr Cotton's she went to the mews in Ellenslea Road to meet her father as he fed his horses and put away his cabs. Maybe they had a row, during which he lost his temper and bludgeoned her with a heavy iron tool used in his trade. Wrapping her in a horse blanket, he may have placed her in (say) a landau and driven to a spot close to the station railings. Cabs were so commonplace, particularly around stations, that it would draw no attention from passers-by, and nobody would take the slightest notice of a cabbie unloading a bundle because dealing with passengers' cases and trunks was part of their job, especially at a seaside resort in August. With the darkness of night helping to provide cover, he could have positioned the cab to shield him from view as he lifted her over the railings.

Thomas was fifty-six, but his job kept him fit and strong enough to carry a girl. Evading Titchener was easy; he had to sweep and clean several rooms on both platforms; whilst he was busy with his indoor chores, Thomas could have surreptitiously carried Polly into the tunnel. On the far end of the up side platform, next to the urinals, was a 7ft high, red-brick, curved wall, behind which anyone descending the embankment would be invisible to station staff. Once at the foot of it, Thomas had only to traverse 10ft of platform, in darkness, save what light the moon supplied, before disappearing into Bopeep Tunnel. His exit was even easier: he need only wait inside the tunnel until Titchener was indoors, then retrace his steps back to the cab.

There is an alleyway running west from the forecourt along the back of the station and around a corner into a shorter alley leading to the up platform. A landau parked at its entrance would attract no attention and its bulk would conceal its driver taking a bundle into the alley. (It is fenced off now, but maybe it was not in 1891.) There were railings at the platform end, but also complete privacy to get a body over them without rushing.

It is possible that Polly was smothered, gassed or drugged before being taken into the tunnel, either unconscious or dead, placed face down between the rails, and bludgeoned. This would account for the 3ft long streak of blood on the track. Her death would be attributed to the head injury, and the head injury blamed on an engine. Dr Colborne said that her head injury was a fatal one, but he did not prove it killed her. Because he thought it had, he most likely did not search for any other cause. He was an ordinary family GP, not a police surgeon or forensic examiner.

❀ ❀ ❀

After Polly died the Sheathers' lives unravelled and their bigamous marriage ended. In 1893 they signed a Deed of Separation: Elizabeth agreed to keep away from him and, in return, he would pay her 10s a week (about £50 today) maintenance. She returned to London, where later that same year she was voluntarily admitted to Islington Workhouse, spending thirteen days in Hagar Ward, which specialised in mental illnesses.

Thomas Sheather lost his neat terraced house and his business, and was reduced to driving a stage carriage (a horse-drawn omnibus). Sinking further he lost his omnibus licence and ended up as a lowly cabbie. He twice fell into arrears with the maintenance payments, and each time Elizabeth sued him in the County Court. On the second occasion, in September 1896, Thomas explained why he had stopped paying: she had 'annulled the deed' by 'annoying' him and calling him names. He brought three witnesses, including Acting Inspector Thomas Jarvis of Hastings Police, to testify that Elizabeth had stated publicly that he murdered his daughter. Nothing seems to have ensued from this astounding allegation.

Elizabeth could have been speaking the truth, or mental illness or alcoholism may have caused her to spout nonsense; she may even have said it just to annoy him. She would not have mentioned murder if she had been involved in Polly's death, especially in front of a police officer, who may have reopened the enquiry on the strength of her words. Two weeks later she appeared at Hastings Magistrates' Court, charged with threatening to 'throttle' a woman in the Norman Hotel.

There are no further records of Elizabeth in St Leonards. The 1901 census shows her scraping a living in Islington as an unqualified monthly nurse. That year, Thomas was fined 10s for being drunk in charge of a horse and trap. During his final years he lived in a room above a stable at 53 Western Road, where he died of cancer in 1907. Records are silent for Elizabeth until 1915, when she died in Islington Workhouse's Highgate Hill Infirmary.

References: 'Estimation of the time of death based on the assessment of post mortem processes with emphasis on body cooling'. *Legal Medicine*: March 2009; *HSLO* 4th March, 29th August & 12th September 1891; 2nd May, 23rd May, 12th September & 3rd October 1896. *Northern Whig* 29th August 1891.

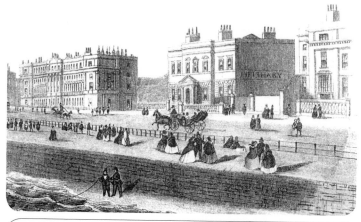

Top: lithograph from about 1860. The infirmary is in the centre.

Centre: lithograph of the East Sussex Hospital. *Illustrated London News* 22nd October 1887.

Above: the handsome new building was constructed of red brick with Portland stone dressings.

INTERLUDE: THE HOSPITALS OPPOSITE HASTINGS PIER

The central Hastings hospital, in its various incarnations, appears in this book several times, so here is a brief overview of how the 1840s infirmary became the 1990s Conquest.

The Hastings & St Leonards Infirmary opened in 1841 on land purchased from the Eversfield Estate for £300. It was then on the edge of Hastings, next to open fields, with a garden on its west side, part of which was later used to build a new wing. Population growth called for a larger establishment, so the infirmary was demolished and replaced in 1887 with the East Sussex Hospital, at a cost of £24,000. Four storeys high, it could accommodate sixty-eight patients in five circular wards of twelve patients each, whilst six wards held only one or two beds each. A lift took patients to a paved roof terrace on top of the circular wards, where patients could enjoy the sunshine. The wards led to wide corridors with unglazed windows, into which less mobile patients could be wheeled, still in their beds, to breathe restorative sea air. These corridors also led to the administrative offices and rooms for the resident medical officer, matron, nurses and servants.

In 1872 the pier opened directly opposite, and each year the number of visitors, vehicles and musical performances increased. The tranquility of the area was destroyed. The hospital had become boxed in by adjacent new buildings, leaving no room for expansion. After fifteen years of discussion, in 1920 the governors secured a site on Cambridge Road and built the Royal East Sussex Hospital, known as the RESH. By 1923 the transfer of equipment and patients was complete and the unique seafront building, just thirty-six years old, was demolished and replaced with the White Rock Pavilion, completed in 1927 and now the White Rock Theatre.

The RESH was closed after the Conquest Hospital was built on the Ridge in 1992. The Cambridge Road site in the image below was cleared and replaced with a modern housing estate.

The site in 1870. The White Rock Brewery is the lower
building on the left, with the Seaside Hotel to its right.

The Palace Hotel around 1890.

1892 • 1900 • 1904

THE CURSE OF THE BONES

THE PALACE HOTEL

Following the removal of an enormous white rock obstructing the road between Hastings and the new town of St Leonards, in 1834–5 the area was redeveloped. The White Rock Brewery and the Seaside Hotel were constructed on the seafront, whilst high on the cliff behind them coastguards' cottages were built on the site of an ancient church called St Michael-on-the-Rock. Cutting back the cliff face accidentally exposed its burial ground, causing a large number of dry, old bones and skulls to tumble down the cliff face to the ground below. Fifty years later, when the brewery and hotel were redeveloped, these same bones were again uncovered and disturbed, this time by builders preparing the foundations for the Palace Hotel.

Some say that spirits seek revenge for such desecration and curse the site in perpetuity.

The Palace Hotel was built for international catering company Spiers & Pond. It opened in 1887 and, after a major upgrade in 1894, became the most luxurious hotel in Hastings, boasting 140 guestrooms or suites, a parade of shops on the ground floor, a 200-seat restaurant, a bar and a tea-room, running hot water, electric lighting and two electro-hydraulic lifts.

It was unusual to site a hotel's kitchen on the fourth storey, but in this instance it was the ideal position. A road on St Michael's cliff behind the hotel provided the perfect spot for suppliers to park their delivery vans. Food, drink and linen was barrowed across a footbridge to the hotel's rear entrance and straight into the kitchen without having to negotiate stairs or lifts. Likewise, all the hotel's refuse was removed discreetly from the rear, rather than via the hotel's elegant public facade.

Hotel kitchens are notorious for becoming too hot and too stuffy, but this one was provided with five sash windows looking out to sea, which let in plenty of cool, fresh air. From time to time a broken sash cord meant a window refused to stay up, and to prop it open staff would grab the nearest suitable utensil. A rectangular metal vegetable strainer proved to be the perfect size and shape for the job .

The hotel's passenger lift was worked by a specific, liveried attendant, but any member of staff could operate the service lift. With skeletal simplicity, it had no door or roof; the cab moved up and down within a tall shaft on a visible pulley system. The shaft was protected by a lattice gate on each storey, which

A paddle steamer at the pier. The Hastings & St Leonards Steamboat Co. carried 95,000 passengers yearly. It owned two splendid, luxuriously-appointed steamboats: the *Alexandra* and the *Britannia*, and between May and September offered day excursions to Eastbourne, Brighton, Newhaven, Dover, Dungeness, Deal, Folkestone and Boulogne.

Beach Terrace, which was demolished in 1931.

could be opened even if the cab was not alongside, an arrangement which today would horrify health and safety inspectors.

Tragically, the luggage lift was to claim the lives of two young servants. The first, Willie Kemp, was a fifteen-year-old pageboy on his tenth day at work, 27th July 1892. The hotel's engineer bellowed up the lift shaft, seeking the 'all clear' to bring the cab down to the basement. Willie leaned forward and looked down into the shaft to call back a reply, not noticing that, above his head, the cab had begun its descent. Its wooden floor struck him a ferocious blow to the skull, knocking him flat on his belly, then trapped him by the neck between the underside of its floor and the lip of the shaft, crushing his throat and completely severing his windpipe.

His workmates released him and rushed him to the nearby hospital, where Dr Rutherford performed an emergency tracheotomy. It was too late: his lungs had filled with blood and he died of asphyxiation. At the inquest, held by coroner Charles Davenport Jones, the jury returned a verdict of 'accidental death', adding that the company must henceforth exhibit printed instructions inside the lift, and not allow new recruits to operate it during the first four weeks of their employment.

On Christmas Eve 1904 Henry Cooper, nineteen, had been a waiter for nine weeks, so was 'qualified' to operate the lift. He used it to get to the fourth floor kitchen. Night had fallen and there was no light inside either cab or shaft. After dropping off a bucket of used tea leaves he slid the iron lattice gate across and stepped forward into the darkness, unaware that, in his brief absence, the cab had been called down to the basement. The poor boy plummeted over fifty feet through the shaft until he crash-landed, with one leg on either side of the t-shaped iron bar above the cab. He dangled there in indescribable agony for a few seconds, then fell to the floor. Colleagues carried him to hospital, where he died of multiple internal injuries.

The name Charles Harcourt Wordsworth may suggest a grandiose, well-heeled, possibly literary gentleman; it was, however, the baptismal name of a working-class boy from Deptford, who worked — as did his father William and 80,000 other souls — at the Royal Arsenal in Woolwich. Charlie, a turner in the small arms factory, was 'a tall young man of very prepossessing manners', and 'a great favourite with those who knew him'. He had just turned twenty-four, and had recently proposed to his long-term sweetheart Clara Barnett, the daughter of a steam engine fitter. The wedding was planned for the following spring.

In August 1900 Clara's cousin Annie Shillibeer treated her twelve-year-old brother to a fortnight's holiday in Hastings, renting a small suite in Saxon House, a boarding establishment at Beach Terrace, in front of Pelham Crescent. Annie invited Clara and Charlie to join them for a week. Being 'in the trade',

Postcard of the Palace Hotel around the turn of the nineteenth century.

The fourth floor kitchen windows, showing the balcony railing that the strainer fell through twice in one day.

The Russian gun at Beach Terrace. It was moved to the museum in 1931 and melted down during the Second World War to be recycled into armaments. Right: paddle steamer destinations.

DAILY Health-Giving EXCURSIONS
By the Splendid Steamship
A L E X A N D R A,
Starting from
HASTINGS, ST. LEONARDS & EASTBOURNE
PIERS.
SATURDAY, JULY 28th.—11.0 and 11.5, to Eastbourne and back. 3.0, Hastings only, to Eastbourne and back.
SUNDAY, JULY 29th.—11.30. Hastings only, Special Cheap Trip to Dover, Deal, and back. 9.30, Hastings to Eastbourne.
MONDAY, JULY 30th.—12.10, 12.15, to Eastbourne and back. 4.0, Hastings only, to Eastbourne and back.
TUESDAY, JULY 31st.—10.15, Hastings only, to Boulogne.
WEDNESDAY, AUGUST 1st. — 10.15, 10.50, to Eastbourne, Brighton, and back. 7.0, 7.30, to Dungeness Lighthouse.
THURSDAY, AUGUST 2nd—11.15. Hastings only, to Eastbourne and back. 3.0, 3.5, to Eastbourne and back. 5.30, Hastings to Eastbourne.
FRIDAY, AUGUST 3rd.—11.0, St. Leonards only, to Boulogne and back.
SATURDAY, AUGUST 4th.—11.0, St. Leonards only to Mid-Channel. 3.0, 3.5, to Eastbourne and back. 7.0, 7.5, to Eastbourne and back.
SUNDAY, AUGUST 5th.—10.0, 10.15, Dover, Deal and back.

doubtless Charlie was fascinated by the Russian gun, captured during the Crimean War (1853–56), that was on display as a trophy on a stone escarpment outside their lodgings.

On Thursday 6th September Clara and Charlie took a 'health-giving excursion' on a paddle steamer from Hastings Pier to Eastbourne. On their return Annie and Willie met them at the landing stage at 9.30pm. The foursome linked arms and chatted merrily along the pier and the promenade until they reached White Rock, where they crossed the road. As they stepped onto the pavement outside the bar beneath the Palace Hotel (where the Pig's Palace is today) Charlie glanced upwards and exclaimed: 'What's that?' Two seconds later a rectangular object dropped from the sky and slammed him on the head, pitching him headfirst into the gutter.

Clara screamed and fell to her knees at his side. As he lay motionless and unresponsive to her words, blood streamed from his nose and ears. After a few minutes Annie pulled her away so that PC Fred Curtis and some bystanders could lift him into a passing van, which they had flagged down to take him to hospital. Sadly, Charlie was beyond medical help. Despite the ministrations of Dr Redmayne, he died half-an-hour later from a brain haemorrhage. The post mortem revealed that his skull had been shattered into twenty pieces.

The object that killed Charlie was retrieved by PC Curtis. It was a galvanised zinc vegetable strainer, resembling a tray but with a perforated base. Measuring 24 inches by 28 inches, it weighed 14lb.

Charlie's parents arrived the next day. They attended the initial inquest hearing, and after he was formally identified they were allowed to take him home to London for burial.

After a week of police enquiries, the inquest resumed on 15th September. Among those present were Chief Constable Baker and legal representatives of Spiers & Pond. The jury visited the hotel to examine the site of the incident and the kitchen window, then returned to the town hall and focussed on finding out who was responsible for Charlie's death.

The coroner questioned the hotel manager and then his kitchen staff, using interpreters to communicate with an Italian pastry cook and a French chef.[1] There were five sash windows in the kitchen and the cord of the one furthest right had snapped a fortnight earlier. The hotel had hundreds of windows and broken cords were so common that a carpenter was called only when half-a-dozen awaited repair. In the meantime, staff would prop the window open.

The kitchen staff recalled the strainer being used from 4th September. At 8.30am on 6th, a porter opened the window without noticing the strainer had been left outside on the balcony. He disturbed it and it slipped through the railings, even though the gap was a mere quarter-inch wider than the strainer. It plummeted fifty feet and clattered heavily onto the pavement. Luckily nobody was walking past at the time. The night porter who retrieved it remarked that it was a dangerous item to use for that purpose. Later that day someone put it back in the window, again it was dislodged and, by sheer fluke, it again slipped through a gap in the railings. This time it killed an innocent passer-by.

The coroner instructed the jury to consider the case 'with a view to criminal proceedings'. If the person responsible knew the strainer had previously fallen out of the window, then he was guilty of manslaughter. However, it was impossible to establish who that person was. After a four-and-a-half hour hearing the jury returned a unanimous verdict of 'accidental death through the negligence of someone in the employ of Spiers & Pond'.

Epilogue: The Curse of the Bones?

During its short existence the Palace Hotel had a disproportionate amount of bad luck. Including a guest who died in his room, there were four deaths in just eight years. In 1900 it emerged that takings were being embezzled by a staff member and, three years later, the hotel's good name was dragged through the mud again when its electrical engineer was caught stealing the housekeeper's savings from a locked drawer in her bedroom.

As a business the Palace left much to be desired. Some years, guest numbers were so low that little or no profit was made. As early as in 1892 the hotel was verging on closure, but it limped along somehow. The end came in

1. It emerged that most of the hotel staff worked ten hours a day, 9am till 3pm and 5pm till 9pm.

1916, when Spiers & Pond went into receivership. Considering the amount of money, time and effort that had been invested to create a magnificent hotel, to fill it with elegant furniture and fittings, and to source the best chefs from across Europe in order to offer superb gastronomic experiences, it is lamentable that it traded for less than thirty years. In 1917 a notice in the *HSLO* announced that the Palace's rosewood and mahogany furniture and expensive rugs were being auctioned, and the building was used to accommodate army personnel.

In 1921 it was sold and converted into mansion apartments. Though the service lift that killed two boys was removed long ago, the antique passenger lift with its lattice doors remains in daily use.

References: *HSLO* 30th May 1885, 30th July 1892, 15 & 22 September 1900, 31st December 1904; *Illustrated London News* 22nd October 1887.

THE EVERSFIELD HOTEL, ST LEONARDS-ON-SEA

St. Leonards-on-Sea & Hastings.

The EVERSFIELD HOTEL

Redecorated and partially refurnished; is the most comfortable; best position; all public rooms facing front; superior cuisine; lift, electric light; moderate tariff.

J. P. BERTEL, *Manager,*

Late Hotel Victoria, London, W.C.

The directors of the Eversfield felt lucky to have hired a manager who previously worked at the Victoria ('the finest hotel in the world') and proudly mentioned it in adverts. *Le Follet,* December 1894.

An advertisement placed in *The Times* on the day of Mr Bertel's funeral: 5th January 1898.

1897 • 1900

Mrs Bertel's Misfortunes

Eversfield Hotel

When the Eversfield Hotel opened in 1885, as 'the largest and best appointed hotel in St Leonards', the directors took the novel step of appointing a female manager. Mary Simpson, a widow, hired her sister and her daughter to keep the books, and another woman as office manager. Under this unusual, all-female team the hotel earned an outstanding reputation for excellence.

When Mrs Simpson resigned in 1893 the vacancy attracted 145 applicants. The directors chose Joseph Bertel, twenty-four, a native of Bohemia (now the Czech Republic), assisted by his English wife Elizabeth, twenty-eight. Despite their youth, by 1897 it was said that 'No hotel in town is better managed in every department'. Its superb cuisine drew special acclaim and attracted wealthy guests, and the Bertels were frequently entrusted to provide extravagant banquets for civic dignitaries. Joseph's social standing was further enhanced when he was initiated into a local Freemasons' lodge on 18th December 1897.

On the last day of 1897 Joseph took a train to Rye. Returning on the 5.25pm in a single, first-class compartment, he lifted a loaded revolver to his head and pulled the trigger. The porter at Ore was 'greatly horrified' when he discovered the ghastly scene. Unable to do anything to help him, he sat with the unconscious man to Hastings, where an ambulance took him to hospital. Further along the seafront, his wife was bustling around the hotel, checking everything was in order for the special New Year's Eve dinner.

A letter in Joseph's pocket, addressed to the coroner, read: 'All I have done lately has gone wrong. I feel my head must have gone wrong, I cannot stand it any longer ... Death is preferable to madness. P.S. If possible break it gently to my wife, who, poor woman, is an angel.' The post mortem revealed a disease of the brain which may have affected his thoughts and behaviour. The jury returned a verdict of 'suicide whilst in an unsound mind'. Joseph was buried in the Borough Cemetery on 5th January 1898, aged just twenty-nine.

Mrs Bertel was asked to stay until the directors found a new manager, but when they saw how well she ran the hotel alone, they offered her the post, and the hotel was once again run by a woman. At the age of just thirty-three she was in sole charge of a major seafront hotel with a £10,000 annual turnover, a remarkable achievement for a woman at that time. After a year, the directors reported that her 'abilities and attention to the business' had increased profits 'in a remarkable manner'.

Two years after Joseph Bertel's death, a second tragedy befell the Eversfield Hotel.

The Eversfield Hotel.

Waygood of Southwark built the lift for the hotel, and boasted about it in adverts. This one showed the pulley system, with an accumulator to the left of the cab.

Menu of a 'sumptuous' banquet provided by the Bertels for the town's dignitaries in 1894. *HSLO.*

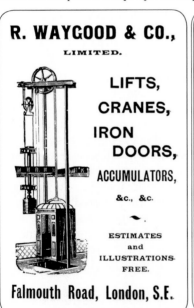
On Tuesday last the Mayor (Alderman Tree) entertained the Recorder, Magistrates, Corporation, Borough Officials, and a few other gentlemen to a sumptuous banquet at the Eversfield Hotel. The gathering passed off most successfully, the proceedings being of a very enjoyable nature. The dinner reflected the highest credit on the hotel and the manager, Mr. J. P. Bertel, a most elegant repast being placed on the tables in a style that elicited unanimous praise. The tables were superbly decorated. We append the *menu* :—

Huîtres.	(Chablis.)
Consommé à la Valantine.	
Crême à la Velours.	(Sherry.)
Filet de Turbot à la Chotsy.	
Escaloppes de Barbue à la Colbert.	(Hock.)
Civet de Lievre à l'Anglaise.	(Chateau.)
Baluntine à la Provencale.	(Margaux.)
Contre Filet de Bœuf à la Pompadour.	(Perrier.)
Panaches à la Printanière.	(Jouet).
Punch à la Romaine.	
Perdreaux et Mauviettes.	
Salade à l'Italienne.	
Pommes Pailles.	(Bollinger. ex. qual. dry.)
Pouding à la Savoisine.	
Gelée à la Diplomate.	(Chateau Leoville.)
Parfait Victoria.	
Canapis à la Dieppoise.	
Dessert.	
Café.	(Liqueurs.)

1900

The Eversfield was the first local hotel to be built with a lift. This secured the patronage of many elderly or infirm visitors who came for the healthy sea air. The advantage was merely temporary, as other large seafront hotels (including the Palace) had them retro-fitted. The lift was maintained by fifty-six-year-old resident engineer Frederick Moore. On the morning of Monday 22nd January he asked luggage porter Lewis Pearson to call it up to the third floor. Finding the latticed gate locked, the lad went to fetch the key. Mr Moore also asked Frederick Streeter, the seventeen-year-old lift attendant, to send the lift up. He tried, but it would go no further than the second floor, so he brought it down again and had another try, but it refused to move. Streeter rang the night porter, Thomas Sampers, and asked him to go and tell Mr Moore what was happening.

Entering the basement engine room Thomas was faced with a gruesome sight: Mr Moore lay dead, crushed beneath the three-ton accumulator. Behind him a stool lay on its side, as though he had been seated when struck from above. It seemed to Thomas that the strap had come off the fork which started the engine wheel, and Mr Moore had been reaching for a spanner to fix it when the huge iron counter-weight descended onto his skull.

Charles Davenport Jones held an inquest later that day. Witnesses described Mr Moore as 'a man of cheerful disposition', much respected by his colleagues and with no troubles. He was a sensible, practical, professional engineer, with eight years' experience of that particular lift, and yet he twice gave instructions for it to be sent up to the third floor whilst he was working beneath the accumulator. The jury was not convinced that his death was accidental. An open verdict was returned because it may have been suicide, even though only a very wicked person would involve a pair of innocent youths and leave one of them to carry the guilt for the rest of his life.

Despite suffering two deeply upsetting fatalities in two years, Mrs Bertel found the courage to remain at the Eversfield. She continued as manager into the twentieth century and went on to hold the post for over twenty-five years. When Queen Victoria died she donated £1 to the fund towards the purchase of a bronze statue, which still stands at the foot of Warrior Square. Hastings Council chose her hotel to host a celebratory banquet lunch for fifty civic dignitaries after the unveiling ceremony on 31st January 1902.

The Eversfield Hotel closed and was converted into flats in the 1960s.

References: *HSLO* 24th February 1894; 9th February 1895; 8th January 1898, 17th February 1900.

HENRY JASPER,

22 & 23, WHITE ROCK (opposite the Band Stand), HASTINGS

JASPER'S BREAD IS THE BEST & MOST DIGESTIBLE.
BAKED BY SPECIAL PROCESS IN HOT-AIR OVENS.

CAKES OF ALL KINDS IN STOCK.
SPECIAL SIZES TO ORDER.
FRESH BUNS, PASTRY, &c., DAILY.

ENGLISH AND FOREIGN SWEETS.
SOUPS, ENTREES, ICES, ETC., SENT OUT.

South Colonnade. Thomas's chemist was the last one on the right.

One of Jasper's many adverts in the *HSLO*.

22–23 White Rock was opposite the bandstand.

1893

FATAL FRIENDSHIP

HAVELOCK ROAD

Frank Singleton Stower's father invented two soft drinks: Stower's Celebrated Orange Tonic Wine and Stower's Lime Juice Syrup. Their enormous popularity ensured that Frank enjoyed a privileged upbringing and a superior private education. When he was nineteen, his world was shattered when his mother was killed, along with twenty-three others, in a catastrophic train crash near Penistone. Soon afterwards his middle-aged father married a woman half his age and started filling the house with babies, so Frank left his Nottinghamshire home to study pharmaceutical chemistry.

In 1892 he became a dispenser at Horace Thomas's long-established chemist shop at 14 South Colonnade, opposite the Undercliff. After a brief stay at Zimmerman's lodging house, he shared a cottage with William and Amelia Goldsmith and their two toddlers at 2 Gensing Road. Frank loved to socialise, and that meant eating and drinking as well as being merry, and he grew 'exceptionally stout' for his age. His other passion was politics and he became a regular at the Central Conservative Club at 31 Havelock Road. Here he met Albert 'Bertie' Jasper and, although Frank was aged twenty-seven, and Bertie only twenty-one, the pair quickly became 'staunch friends' and 'regular chums'.

Bertie was also the son of a successful businessman: Henry Jasper, a well known and highly esteemed master baker with a chain of shops, including two in Hastings. After serving his apprenticeship, in August 1892, when Bertie was just twenty-one, his father placed him in charge of his thriving bakery and shop at 22–23 White Rock, and Bertie moved into the flat above.

Within a year Frank was bored with working in a shop. Fancying a complete change and a bit of adventure, he landed a job as travel companion to a rich gentleman who was taking a trip to the South of France. They would leave on 27th December. He resigned from his job and decided to spend his final week back at Miss Zimmerman's at 43 Havelock Road, where he took a small suite comprising bedroom and sitting room. His former landlady was glad to welcome him back, as she had 'never had a more thoughtful or considerate' guest. When Bertie visited she noticed the pair were 'on very good terms'; in fact Frank treated him like 'a petted younger brother'. Bertie stayed with Frank over Christmas so they could spend some time together before he left.

On Boxing Day the friends spent the evening at the nearby Conservative Club. Late that night they chatted in the front parlour for a while, then went up to bed, 'apparently in perfectly good health and spirits'.

46 (left) and 45 Havelock Road. Nos. 44 and 43 were identical and to the right, where the modern block is. During the Second World War, Havelock Road was hit by a bomb which destroyed nos. 44 to 32. The site was used to build a GPO telephone exchange, which was later converted into a college. The street number 43 has been reallocated; it is not on the site of the original.

The next morning Frank began his final day in Hastings before sailing on the overnight steam ferry to France. At 8.15am he rang for Miss Zimmerman and told her they might skip breakfast and lunch. He and Bertie had taken morphia for insomnia and, as his pal was not accustomed to it, he might sleep all day. She advised drinking plenty of fluids to flush it out of their systems. Whilst she fetched a syphon of soda water and a pot of tea, he composed a telegram to William Holt, inviting him round that evening for a farewell drink. His landlady took it to the nearby post office in Queen's Road.

Although she knew Frank was a qualified pharmacist, Miss Zimmerman could not stop worrying about Bertie. She put her ear to the door several times, and twice heard someone draw soda water. Just before 1pm both were snoring loudly. At 2pm all was silent. She knocked but there was no response. After trying to rouse them at 4.15 and again at 4.30, she was getting quite worried, but, as a woman, she would never enter a man's room whilst it was occupied. She decided to ask Worsley John Harris, a young doctor who lived next door at no.44, to go in and make sure they were all right. He was out so she waited in her bay-windowed front parlour until he got home at 6pm. She took him up then waited anxiously as he, too, knocked and obtained no response. He turned the handle and entered, but the moment he saw two men laying in bed together, naked and motionless, he turned on his heel and swiftly shut the door behind him. Sending Miss Zimmerman to the police station, he examined the bodies. Clearly, both men had been dead for hours.

The younger, slimmer man lay on the right side of the bed, on his back, his face drained of colour, his lips livid red and his body cold as stone. The stouter man lay beside him, on his side, with his knees drawn up to his stomach and his head thrown back. Froth issued from his mouth and there was vomit on the sheet. His skin was deathly white, his muscles were rigid and his hands were clenched 'as if his death had been a harder one'.

Looking around the room the doctor saw tea, brandy, soda water and a jar of marmalade. White powder (that later proved to be morphia) was scattered in a drawer and on the floor by the bed; more was found wrapped in silver paper. Dr Harris gathered up sixteen grains. An empty pill box bore a red label with the inscription: 'Aconite, most deadly poison'. The box had at one time been fastened with string and sealed, and had the name of Frank's former employer, 'Thomas & Co., St. Leonards' printed on it. In a Gladstone bag were eight silver-coated pills in a box marked 'Poison' and a small bottle containing a few drops of chlorodyne, the principal ingredients of which were a mixture of laudanum (an alcoholic solution of opium), tincture of cannabis, and chloroform.

Detective Sergeant Gower arrived at 6.30pm and searched Bertie's clothing, which lay at the end of the bed. In a waistcoat pocket was a silver watch with a gold chain, and in the trousers 2s 4d, a bunch of keys, a cigar cutter and a handkerchief. In the breast pocket of the coat was a short love poem.

Melanethon Moore, a photographer residing at 21 White Rock, next door to Jasper's bakery, arrived, accompanied by Walter Kelsey, an employee of the Jaspers. Then William Holt turned up, expecting a jolly evening with his pals. Everybody stood in stunned silence, shocked at the deaths of two vibrant young men with everything to live for.

The bodies were removed to the mortuary at Rock-a-Nore, where on 29th December Dr Harris conducted the post mortems. He established that Frank died of aconite poisoning and Bertie from an overdose of morphia.

What with police coming and going and bodies being carried out onto police litters, gossipping tongues were wagging from one end of Havelock Road to the other. Rumours spread and soon the whole town was whispering and asking questions, but the *HSLO* was not published for another two days so nobody could get any hard facts, apart from a brief news snippet in Friday's *Sussex Agricultural Express*. The *HSLO*'s lengthy report began:

SENSATIONAL DOUBLE TRAGEDY AT HASTINGS.
TWO FRIENDS FOUND DEAD SIDE BY SIDE.

The inhabitants of Hastings and St Leonards were shocked … by the report of a sensational and distressing double tragedy of singular and mysterious character, the two principals in the melancholy event being two young men of good position, who were stated to have been found dead together in bed, under peculiarly sad circumstances … To a great extent the affair is shrouded in mystery.

In Bertie's case, suicide was 'entirely out of the range of probability' because 'he was the beloved son of a kind-hearted father of affluent means'. He had taken a drug to which he was unaccustomed, with 'fatal effect', whilst Frank, 'driven by grief' at his death, took a dose of 'some more deadly poison'.

Speculation would end once the facts were revealed at the inquest, which was held on 6th January 1894 under Charles Davenport Jones.[1] The Market Hall was crowded to capacity. Frank's sister, a hospital nurse, stated that the drugs he possessed (morphia, chlorodyne and aconite) were used to treat his insomnia and neuralgia. His former landlady said that he was tormented by sleep deprivation and had once remarked on 'How nice it would be to take something to make one sleep and not wake again, so that one might die without pain'.

The coroner suggested that, realising he had accidentally killed his friend, Frank committed suicide by taking aconite. The jury was unconvinced

1. Welshman Charles Davenport Jones (1844–1908) appears in several subsequent chapters. He was a wealthy solicitor who settled in Hastings in 1872 and served as borough coroner from 1877 to 1908. He lived at 30 St Helen's Road and later in a house in Godwin Road which he named *Bryn-y-Mor,* where he died.

and returned an open verdict on his death. They decided that Bertie had died from an overdose of morphia, but there was no evidence to show how it was administered.

Both families must have been relieved by the verdicts. Far better to have the deaths recorded as accidental and not suicidal, or, worse, manslaughter or murder and suicide. They must have been grateful that there was no speculation about why two young men were naked in bed together, and they were perhaps lucky that the text of the love poem was never revealed.

Frank Stower's funeral on 2nd January reeked of shame. Considering the family's wealth it was insultingly modest, and of his family only his father, stepmother and one sister attended. It was telling that all three of his brothers stayed away. Nor did the Stower family care to take his body home to Nottingham; instead they left him in the Borough Cemetery, where his grave would be left unattended and too distant for anyone to visit.

Bertie's funeral was completely different: his body was taken home to Strood, and he was given a grand send-off. The Jaspers were well known locally because of their bakeries, and business owners and shop workers came to show their respects. His coffin was covered with lavish floral tributes — including a handsome cross made of flowers from the bakers and shop workers at White Rock — and was processed slowly through the streets in a glass-sided hearse drawn by black-plumed horses and followed by eight mourners' carriages. As the cortège passed, 'many of the shops showed signs of sorrow' by dropping their blinds or closing their shutters. Bertie was interred in the family grave, under a tall pedestal bearing a large and costly carved stone figure of an angel.

Miss Zimmerman was so traumatised by the incident that she closed her lodging house, moved elsewhere and lived a quiet life until her death in 1905. She leased 43 Havelock Road to a veterinary surgeon, who used it as his home and surgery.

References: *Sussex Agricultural Express* 29th December 1893; *HSLO* 30th December 1893 & 6th January 1894.

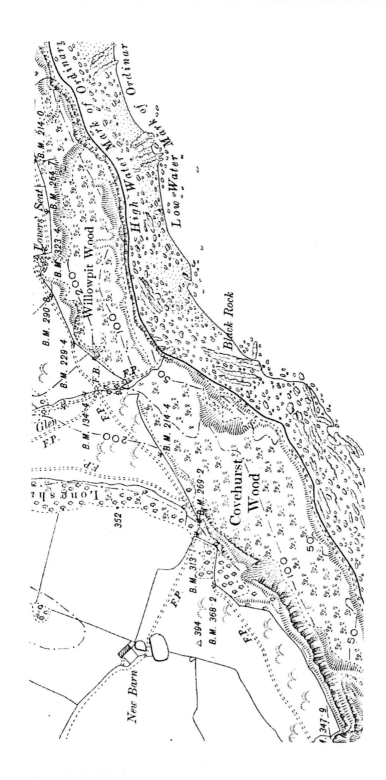

1896

Look Before you Leap

Covehurst Wood

On Sunday 20th June a dozen pals set off on a jolly boys' outing to the picturesque cliffs between the glens of Ecclesbourne and Fairlight. It was not the scenery that attracted them but the isolation: they intended to play cards. Even though the men bet mere farthings and halfpennies, gambling was illegal, so subterfuge was required. They selected a spot due south of the New Barn, at the western edge of Covehurst Wood. The fine summer's morning attracted many hikers, picnickers and ramblers, with their many pairs of prying eyes. The men climbed over the fence — erected to prevent daft tourists from falling to their deaths — to a wide strip of ground between the fence and the cliff edge. It was chalky, grassy, and dotted with clumps of bushes. Finding a small clearing, they settled themselves down for a morning's amusement.

The East Sussex Constabulary had received a number of tip-offs about illegal card schools in the area. It had a presence at Fairlight in the shape of Constable Baldwin, who had been posted there specifically to 'prevent nuisances caused by rough people'; in other words to protect genteel visitors from being pestered by the poor, who were forever begging, pressure-selling trinkets, purporting to tell fortunes or reciting romantic stories of the Lovers' Seat, in the hope of receiving a penny. PC Baldwin had been given the additional task of putting a stop to illegal gambling. No arrests were to be made; the men were simply to be informed that their actions were illegal, issued with a stern warning, and asked for their names, both to keep a record and to scare them sufficiently to prevent a recurrence of the offence.

On 20th June Baldwin spotted a group of men walking south across Cliff Field. Because they had dogs he took them for poachers, so he called at Little Warren Cottage to invite the gamekeeper, Tom Barnes, to accompany him. As they approached the fence they heard voices and the chink of coins. Clearly, they were not poachers, but gamblers. With Barnes leading, the pair quietly climbed the fence and sneaked along the short path to a clearing. Seeing about a dozen men, some standing, some sitting, Barnes remarked jocularly, 'This is a pretty party'. The men, seeing Baldwin's police helmet and uniform, instantly took fright; hats and cards were 'flung about' wildly as they 'fled in all directions'. Two ran towards the cliff edge; one hid in a bush, whilst the other 'made three distinct leaps' over big clumps of furze. Barnes, acutely aware of the danger, shrieked at him: 'Don't jump, for goodness' sake! You'll be over the cliff!' but by the time he finished saying it, the man had vanished.

The cliffs to the east of Hastings.

On the beach below the cliff Henry Brett gasped in horror as he watched the figure of a man plummet one hundred feet, then bounce off a ledge before continuing to free-fall till he crash-landed on the ragged stones with a sickening thud. No man could possibly survive such a fall, so Brett did not approach the body; 'I hadn't a heart to', he later explained. He raised the alarm and Dr Joseph Hooker was summoned from his home to pronounce life extinct. The police conveyed the battered body to an outhouse on Fishponds Farm.

The corpse was indentified as that of John Towner. His death 'created a painful sensation in the borough, particularly in the Old Town' because he was only twenty-eight and, moreover, was the father of three small children, all under five years of age. Although John was a bricklayer, his father had been a boatman for many years and his brother served in the Royal Navy, so 'the flags of the fishing boats and other craft were flown at half-mast', because they considered John to be one of their own.

An inquest was held the next day in a makeshift coroner's court at Fishponds farmhouse, under Charles Sheppard, who was coroner for the Rape of Hastings for fifty-four years. After viewing the scene of the accident, the jury was hearing from the witnesses when John Towner's father interrupted and demanded an adjournment. He accused Tom Barnes of pushing his son over the cliff edge, and, if given two weeks to assemble witnesses, he would prove it. The coroner told him to sit down and not interrupt 'in this unseemly manner'. If he could prove his allegation, then he must take up the matter with the police after the inquest.

The next witness was bathchair man Joe Tredree, aged forty-eight. He was a former boatman of the coastguard, an occupation that earned instant respect; moreover, he was the recipient of a medal for long service and good conduct. In Hastings, the word of such a man was 'the gospel truth'. After a Sunday morning stroll in Covehurst Wood he sat down on a slope for a well-earned rest. From this elevated vantage point he had witnessed the 'raid' and was absolutely certain that Barnes did not go within 15ft of young John Towner. The father's assertion was also contradicted by one of his son's friends and fellow card players, George Burgess of Harold Road, who confirmed that Tredree's statement was true.

The coroner summed up: John Towner, whilst illegally gambling, was startled by the sudden appearance of two officials and made off in a panic. It was a dangerous spot in which to be running about carelessly, and he did not realise the consequences of what he was doing when he leapt over the bushes. The jury's verdict was 'death by misadventure'.

Six days later John Towner senior and Joe Tredree had a 'free and frank exchange of views' near the Dun Horse in Albion Street, Halton. Towner accused Tredree of giving false evidence, then slugged him in the mouth with a clenched fist, sending him sprawling across the pavement. Mr Tredree reported the assault to a passing policeman. Towner was summonsed to the magistrates' court and fined ten shillings plus costs.

John Towner left his widow penniless, with three small children, and no means of support. Three neighbours from Priory Road, plus a benevolent dairyman from Bachelor's Bump, started a subscription fund to save them from the workhouse. In just a few weeks they raised the equivalent of over £2,000. By 1901 Annie and her children were lodging with a family and scraping a living as a daily domestic servant. Four years later she was dead, and her children, then fourteen, twelve and nine, became orphans.

References: *Sussex Agricultural Express* 23rd June 1896; *Bexhill Observer* 27th June 1896; *HSLO* 27th June, 4th July & 1st August 1896.

Pelham Crescent with Pelham Arcade in front, built by Joseph Kay in 1824-8. The arcade was an early, purpose-built shopping arcade, which formed part of a complex that included seawater baths and a bazaar. No.8 is next door to the 'mail carts and prams' shop with the awning. These photos were taken after Mr Neal's shop was (rather ironically) replaced with a rifle range.

The *Shoreditch Observer* marking the sale of Rose Neal & Son. Note how the reporter used the term 'tradesmen' and 'Messrs', meaning 'gentlemen' for the female-led firm.

AN OLD ESTABLISHED FIRM.—The business carried on for over 43 years in Mare-street, opposite the Grove, by Messrs. Rose Neal and Son, has been purchased by Messrs. C.W. Felgate and Co. As wholesale and retail wine merchants, the old firm received a large amount of patronage for many years, and now that the business has come into the hands of Messrs. Felgate, they have shown their usual enterprise, in remodelling the cellars and bottling departments, and in modernising the frontage in Mare-street. The present proprietors are well known for their mature judgment and high integrity as Hackney tradesmen, and there is no doubt the business will extend yet further under their spirited management.

1899

THE MYSTERY OF THE MISSING GUN

PELHAM ARCADE

Charles Neal was the grandson of John Nash, a bookseller at the Pantiles in Tunbridge Wells in the 1790s, and the son of Rose Nash and Thomas Neal. His father's business ventures, both as a linen draper and as a wine merchant, ended in bankruptcy. After his early death Rose revived the wine business in Hackney and took Charles into partnership. 'Rose Neal & Son' was hugely successful, and when Rose sold it in 1883 the hefty sale price guaranteed them both a comfortable retirement.

Rose died in 1897. Charles was almost sixty and had never lived apart from her. Having inherited the equivalent of nearly half-a-million pounds he had no need to earn; nevertheless he became a shopkeeper, first in Southend, then in Hastings, where he took over an established tobacconist at 8 Pelham Arcade. As well as cigarettes, cigars, pipes, loose tobacco and matches, it sold newspapers, umbrellas and walking sticks, but still made so modest a profit that the chief constable would later describe it as 'not worth troubling about'.

On Saturday 16th December 1899 Mr Neal's errand boy Tommy Dabson, seventeen, arrived for work at 8.45am. The front door was ajar but his boss was not his usual place behind the counter. Tommy called his name and looked in the store rooms. He found his boss lying on the floor, motionless. PC George Burr was across the road, so he went out and called him over.

Burr sent Tommy to fetch a doctor whilst he examined the scene. Mr Neal lay face down, his head in a pool of blood, unconscious but breathing. His right arm was bent underneath his torso, tightly clutching a pair of spectacles, and his left arm lay by his side. The only blood was beneath his head, there was no sign of a struggle and, most interestingly, no gun. Mr Neal was dressed for winter in overcoat, boots, trousers, a jacket and two waistcoats. A bloodstained hat lay eighteen inches from him. His pockets contained no house or shop keys, just £3 3s in cash and an expensive gold watch and chain.

The front door, the only way into the shop, was fitted with a Yale-type latch and a deadlock. Both were in perfect order and the door had not been forced open. At the rear a series of skylights ran along the entire arcade, with windows to ventilate each shop. Mr Neal's was securely fastened from the inside. After he was taken to hospital PC Burr and Detective Sergeant Thomas Coppard searched every inch of the premises for a weapon, to no avail.

Mr Neal died at 6pm. The post mortem showed that the bullet wound was such that he would have lost consciousness immediately. He would not have been able to dispose of or hide a gun.

At the inquest the witnesses could think of no motive for suicide or murder. Mr Neal's cousin William Delves, an accountant and magistrate in Tunbridge Wells, described him as a 'quiet, temperate man' who was solitary to the point of eccentricity. The shop was leased, the stock was cheap, and he lived frugally. However, in just two years Mr Neal had withdrawn from his bank three-quarters of his £650 inheritance (£487, the equivalent of over £200,000 today) and his accounts did not show where it had gone.

The focus shifted to Mr Neal's final hours. Charles Gallop of 8 Gordon Road, was the last person to see him alive when he visited the shop at about 8.30pm. John Hughes, of 6 Pelham Crescent, went to the door at about 9.15pm, but found the shop closed, in darkness and silent.

The police gave special attention to lock-up shops because the owners did not live above them. PC Brockwell, on no.2 beat from 10pm to 6am and had passed 8 Pelham Arcade at 10.25pm. He saw a light inside, which was not unusual. Passing again at 12.40am the light was off. He tried the door and it was locked. The skylight window was closed and screwed up tightly on the inside. Between 12.40 and 8am the shops' front doors were checked every hour-and-a-half; however, on that day they were not checked after 5.40 because twenty-one officers due on duty at 6am were off sick with influenza.

Shop assistant Jessie Clarke last saw Mr Neal when she left work at 7pm the night before he died. The day's takings were £3 10s, most of which was found on Mr Neal the next morning. Arriving at 10am the next morning Tommy told her Mr Neal had 'had a fit' and was in hospital. Mr Neal always kept the front door keys in the till, but they were missing. When asked if Mr Neal was left-handed, Jessie recalled that he weighed loose cigarettes right and left-handed, so he could probably pull a trigger with either hand.

The police needed a home address for Mr Neal, to search it for clues and inform whoever he lived with of his death, but Jessie could not help. He told her how much he enjoyed his 15 minutes' walk to work, but not where he lived. He once gave Tommy twenty-eight detachable shirt collars for his mother to launder, but told him to return them to the shop. Tommy said that one of the store rooms 'smelled very close' in the mornings. PC Burr found a comb and brush, boot brushes and blacking, cooking utensils and a gas stove, two pails, some dirty linen, and greasy marks on a wall. Clearly, Mr Neal had been sleeping there. Why an elderly man with ample funds chose to sleep on the cold, hard floor of a store room, without sanitation or home comforts, was a mystery all of its own, especially as a warm, comfortable single room could be rented nearby for a mere 5s a week.

Arthur King deposed that when he worked as a bicycle mechanic at Herbert Kingston's, 5 Pelham Arcade, he would visit Mr Neal after hours. In October Mr Neal showed him a brand new .32 bore revolver he had acquired. King omitted to explain why Mr Neal bought it, or why he showed it to him, nor whether it was the reason he ceased their friendship shortly afterwards. King

A .32 revolver similar to
that supposedly owned
by Charles Neal.

claimed it was because he no longer worked at the arcade; however, he lived within five minutes' walk.

The coroner remarked that the only certainty about the case was that Mr Neal died from a bullet in the brain. The remainder 'resolved itself into possibilities and probabilities'. Under his direction the jury returned an open verdict. The police carried on making enquiries; however, newspapers fell silent about the case and the mysterious death of Mr Neal remains unsolved.

Suicide was ruled out because no gun was found, but what if someone had taken it? Tommy Dabson's father and uncle were police officers; perhaps that spurred the boy to be interested in crime and weapons, and when he found Mr Neal (he thought) 'having a fit', he spotted a gun, snatched it up on impulse and hid it (somewhere outdoors) whilst PC Burr searched the shop. After he found out Mr Neal died of a gunshot wound, he may have felt too ashamed to admit to taking it, fearing the legal consequences and his father's undoubted wrath for 'interfering with evidence'. Then in a panic he disposed of it, so effectively that it was never found. Of course, this fails to explain why the keys were missing.

If the above scenario is incorrect, Charles must have been murdered. The killer shot him and left, taking the gun and the keys. By all accounts nobody bore him a grudge. His only friend, Arthur King, had just dropped him, so it is worth examining their strange friendship.

At the inquest King stated that, between mid-1898 and October 1899, he 'spent two or three evenings in the week, and sometimes every evening' alone with Mr Neal in the store rooms behind his shop. Neither the coroner nor the newspapers remarked on what King, aged twenty-five and Neal, sixty-one, were doing together for so many hours a week in such bleak surroundings, devoid of the smallest home comfort or amusement. The shop was surrounded by warm, cheerful public houses, dining rooms, comfortable hotel lounges and clubs to suit all tastes and pockets. Why did they only meet in the shop? They must have been doing something illicit.

In the 1890s homosexual acts were illegal and the penalties severe, so strict secrecy was paramount. Given the age difference, a love affair seems less likely than Neal paying King for his 'favours'. However, the 'business' would be transacted in minutes, not hours, especially in such comfortless surroundings. What were they doing for the rest of the time?

DEATH KEEPS THE SECRET.

What is believed to be a crime of a cowardly character was investigated on Monday at Hastings. An elderly tobacconist, Mr. Charles Henry Weil, of 8, Pelham Arcade, was discovered lying in his shop in a pool of blood, unconscious. The shop door, which had been securely fastened on the previous night was ajar. The old man bore a severe wound on the left side of the head. He never recovered consciousness, but died the same day.

THE HASTINGS MYSTERY.

———:0:———

TOBACCONIST'S STRANGE DEATH.

———

SUICIDE OR MURDER?

———

WHERE THE DECEASED LIVED.

———

BULLET IN THE BRAIN.

———

BUT NO PISTOL FOUND.

The skylight on top of Pelham Arcade.

News story in the *Monmouthshire Beacon*

Headlines in the *HSLO*.

I believe they were gambling, probably at cards, but maybe also halma, backgammon and mah-jong. Neal may have been addicted to games, or to gambling, or both, and King may have been a shrewd confidence trickster. He could have gained Neal's trust by ensuring that Neal won at gambling games more than half the time, and always paying up promptly and graciously when he lost. In this way he built a reputation as an honourable man. As they played, King chatted casually about investments, impressing Neal with his financial acumen, and speaking of stock market killings made by his (imaginary) chum, brother or cousin 'in the City'.

After weeks or months he would have Neal's total trust and confidence, and could proceed to the next step. He revealed to Neal that his chum in the City, who had 'insider knowledge', had given him the tip-off to invest heavily in some 'surefire' venture — a trust, stock or share, oil, gold or diamond mine — which was 'guaranteed' to double in price. King could have faked being deeply frustrated at having only a few pounds to invest, saying if he were rich he would go 'all in'. If King had laid his groundwork correctly, there would be no need to cajole Neal to invest; the naive old man would have practically begged King to persuade his 'chum in the City' to invest his money. Neal was thus divested of between £100,000 and £200,000, paid in cash to King, to be passed on to his City chum. Eventually King broke the bad news that the investment had collapsed and both he and Neal had lost everything.

Neal somehow discovered or realised he had been scammed and demanded the return of his money. King ceased to visit and resigned from his job to avoid him. Neal threatened to go to the police, so King promised to bring the money to him at the shop, or discuss the matter, on Saturday 16th December, early in the morning before the shop opened. When Neal let him in, King shot him, and when he left he had to turn the mortice key in the lock to get out. He pocketed the keys just in case the police could somehow trace who had unlocked the door by the fingerprints on the keys. He then turned up at the inquest to tell a tall tale about Neal owning a gun.

This wild speculation could be completely wrong.

I traced Mr King's subsequent life, using genealogical sites. He enjoyed a comfortable, middle-class lifestyle, not fabulously wealthy but certainly not poor, and much better off than he should have been as a humble bicycle mechanic. Both he and his wife left tidy sums in their wills.

References: *Maidstone Journal* 6th May 1851; *Lloyd's List* 8th January 1876; *Shoreditch Observer*, 23rd August, 1883; *Sussex Agricultural Express* 23rd December 1899; *HSLO* 6th January 1900.

John Bray offering the shop for sale on 13th January 1900.

TOBACCONIST'S BUSINESS, carried on at No. 8, Pelham Arcade, Hastings, with Stock and Fittings, to be sold with immediate possession.—Apply, John and A. Bray, Business Agents, White Rock, Hastings.

The path that once led from Braybrooke Road to the foot crossing.

The dotted black line indicates the path across the railway.

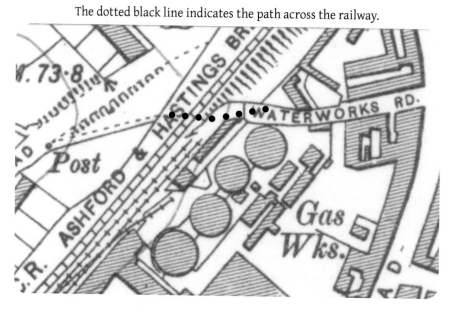

1900

THE FINAL CROSSING

WATERWORKS ROAD

From birth to death Helen Taylor's life was dominated by the railway. Before she was born her father was an official at Spa Road on London's first line, the London & Greenwich Railway, which opened in 1836. Later he became a station master, and his children grew up in the station houses at Erith and Gravesend. In 1865, when she was sixteen, Helen's heart filled with pride as the Royal Train stopped on the platform outside their home and she watched her father open a carriage door for the Prince of Wales.

Living on a station, the Taylors' everyday life was dictated by the railway, its routines, timetables, rules and customs. Helen's brother became a station master and she married the son of the station master at Rye. Her children grew up in station houses because her husband, William Hunt, was also a station master, first at Robertsbridge and then at Ramsgate. Her brother died in railway service: in 1892 he shot himself dead in his office at Cliffe station, leaving his young wife to raise their small daughter alone.

In January 1900 the Hunts and their five youngest children moved to Hastings, because William had been appointed station superintendent, at a yearly salary of £250 (£26,000 today). This time, his workplace had no station house; instead he was paid a rent allowance, which he used to lease 84 Braybrooke Road. The ten-roomed villa was perched on top of a hill behind one of the signalboxes, and its rear windows afforded a bird's eye view of the sprawling station, its platforms, sheds and sidings.

Opposite the corner of Braybrooke Road and Lower Park Road there used to be a public footpath that led across the railway line to Waterworks Road. Known informally as 'gasworks' or 'waterworks' crossing, it provided a short cut to the shops in Queen's Road. Such arrangements were common in those days; there were only two tracks and they were not yet electrified; the line speed was 15mph and enginemen would toot their horns twice as they emerged from Ore Tunnel, giving ample time for anyone walking across to get clear.

On 5th April 1900 William Hunt had barely arrived home at 8pm when a messenger brought the sad news that someone had been run over at the public foot crossing. He returned to the station to take charge of the incident and find out exactly what happened before taking a cab to the mortuary to view the body. Walter Lewell, driver of the 6.55pm from Ashford, had hit 'something white' at the crossing. All signals were turned to danger, all trains were stopped, and young Porter Turner was despatched to examine the line. He discovered an awful sight: a woman was on the track, cut up by a train's wheels. She was beyond help, so Turner returned to the station.

The police surgeon, George Locke of 47 Wellington Square, arrived at the crossing at 8pm. The woman was 'completely severed at the trunk' and her right arm had been sliced off. She had apparently lain across a rail on the down line, one arm folded under her chest, and her hat, umbrella and shawl lay close by, as if placed deliberately. The corpse was conveyed to the mortuary at Rock-a-Nore where Mr Hunt identified her: she was his wife.

Whilst Mr Hunt broke the devastating news to his children, the youngest of whom was only eight, Dr Locke conducted a post mortem. The position of the body had led him to suspect she had committed suicide, and his examination found a 'long standing mischief in the brain'.

Coroner Charles Davenport Jones held an inquest at the Market Hall in George Street on 8th April. Mr Hunt explained that, when he arrived home after Helen was found, he saw a note in her handwriting which read, 'Gone for walk in the Park'. She did not need to cross the railway to reach the park, so must have taken a wrong turning. Hunt hoped her death would be recorded as an accident, though he knew that someone who had lived on railway stations for half a century could not wander naively onto a line and ignore two long, loud warning whistles from a slow moving steam engine.

Mrs Hunt's GP stated that she suffered from epilepsy, and although she had been depressed, that was in the past. Her family claimed that she had 'delusions', and he had written to her former GP for more information. The coroner invited the jury to 'join with him in offering to Mr Hunt their sincere sympathy in his painful loss'. The verdict was the only one that fitted the evidence: 'suicide whilst temporarily insane'.

Mrs Hunt was buried in the Borough Cemetery without a church service. The Rev. Dr Finnemore officiated at the graveside in the presence of Mr Hunt and his four eldest sons, aged between thirteen and twenty. His daughters, who were seventeen and eight, did not attend. Many floral tributes were received, including from the railwaymen at Ramsgate and Hastings stations.

The death of Helen Hunt prompted Hastings Council to hold several meetings to discuss abolishing the foot crossing, and in 1902 they passed a resolution to ask the railway company to replace it with an underpass a few yards to the east. This led to a formal public petition, followed up by a specific request that the new 'foot tunnel' be lined with glazed white bricks and lit by electricity. Despite this great flurry of activity, it took thirteen years for the railway to comply. The underpass they built is still in use today.

Epilogue: William Hunt

Despite his wife's death in such a horrific manner, Mr Hunt stayed in his post as superintendent at Hastings. His two eldest sons were already railway clerks, two

Looking south through the underpass which replaced the crossing.

more joined the industry as soon as they left school: Percival as an apprentice engine fitter and Harold as a parcels clerk.

Soon after Helen died Mr Hunt married a local widow, but within a year she was bedridden with a terminal illness from which she died in 1903. He did not marry again. In 1908 he was promoted to the prestigious post of station superintendent at Victoria. At his crowded farewell party, held in Hastings station's main waiting room, many heartfelt eulogies were raised. Staff presented him with a 'handsomely chased and engraved silver salver, as a token of the high esteem in which they held him', and in his speech Mr Hunt hoped he was 'not saying good-bye to them forever' (which proved to be prophetic). His sons moved with him to London, but his daughters stayed in Hastings, sharing rented rooms at 4 Cambridge Road.

In 1914 Mr Hunt retired and moved back to Hastings, but just weeks later the Great War began and he was re-engaged to perform 'secret work'— probably managing the provision of troop trains for the government, which had taken control of the railways for the duration of the war. In 1919, aged sixty-seven, he was appointed temporary station master during a national railway strike. He retired for the second time in 1920, having completed an impressive fifty-five years in railway service. He died four years later at his home, 17 Linton Road.

References: *HSLO* 6th & 13th April 1900; 23rd November 1902; 21st March 1908; 6th March 1915.

The second coastguard station at Ecclesbourne.

The first station at Ecclesbourne was built on the beach at the foot of the glen in 1819. From the start, the coastguards and their families lived on the premises. A storm in 1859 damaged the station so badly that a replacement, with more commodious accommodation, was built on the cliff, with a steep path leading down to wooden steps giving access to the beach and the boats.

Looking west over the coastguard station towards Hastings over the rising cliffs.

1904

FOR THE WANT OF A POCKET

ECCLESBOURNE

Frederick Jackson was born in Devon in 1873. He joined the Royal Navy at fifteen and served on ships for sixteen years until, in April 1904, he was seconded by the Admiralty to be a boatman at Ecclesbourne. Three months later, on Friday 1st July, his boss, Chief Boatman Walter Martin, handed Frederick his month's salary in the form of postal orders in his name. The men were always paid that way to save them carrying large sums of money, and they would cash them as required. In the evening Mr Martin gave Frederick permission to go shopping, so long as he was back by 10pm. On his way back to Ecclesbourne at about 9pm Frederick ran into a colleague in Tackleway and, telling him he had forgotten something, he turned back and visited Carrie Ticehurst's eating-house at 14 Courthouse Street, where he bought half-a-dozen saveloys.

Frederick failed to return that night, but he was not on duty until the morning so Martin gave him a bit of leeway. When he was still not back by the time his watch duty started at 6am, Martin sent out a search party. Despite searching the cliffs all the way to Hastings, they found no trace of him.

About 8am holidaymakers walking along the shore spotted a man lying on a ledge part-way up the 200-foot cliff face. They observed him for a few minutes and, seeing no movement, reported their concerns to the coastguard. Rescuers found Frederick dead. Scattered about on the ledge were his cap, a postal order for £5 10s, seven shillings and sixpence in silver and threepence-halfpenny in coppers, a matchbox containing two sovereigns and two half-sovereigns, and two saveloys.

Police wheeled the body to the mortuary in a litter[1] and Police Surgeon Henry G. Shorter conducted the post mortem. Frederick had died from a broken neck, and there was no sign of intoxication.

The inquest was held by Coroner Charles Davenport Jones at the Market Hall in George Street, to establish if the deceased had jumped, fallen, or was pushed. People were kept away from the cliff edge by a fence, and between the fence and the edge was an irregular strip of grass averaging twenty feet wide. The area had been inspected, the fence was upright and intact, and the grass above the ledge where Frederick was found showed no sign of a struggle. In any case, Mr Martin stated that Frederick was 'a very powerful man', and 'six men could not have put him over the fence' against his will. Mr Martin also said

---

1. A wooden hand-cart with a flat platform and large wheels.

The pocketless uniform of H.M. coastguard

that Frederick had no reason to kill himself; he was 'a very steady man' with a spotless naval service record. However, Mr Martin had a theory that might provide an explanation for Frederick's seemingly inexplicable fall.

Boatmen's uniforms had been designed without pockets, and the men were in the habit of placing small valuables such as letters, money and postal orders into the band of their caps. The night of 1st July had been extremely blustery; perhaps a particularly strong gust of wind had whipped off Frederick's cap and blown it over the fence, complete with his precious cash and postal orders. He may have climbed over the fence to retrieve it and, in the pitch black of the moonless night, with the cliff edge being jagged and therefore unpredictable, and with him not yet being completely familiar with the area, and panicking about the loss of a month's wages, Frederick tumbled over the cliff edge.

The jury returned a verdict of 'accidental death'.

On 6th July fifty coastguards followed Frederick's hearse to the Borough Cemetery. Most came from Bexhill, Rye and Pett; a handful travelled from further afield, to pay their respects to their brother. There was an escort of eighteen men, some of whom acted as pall-bearers. Frederick's coffin was wrapped in the Union Jack and, at the graveside, three volleys were fired. Townspeople, most of whom had never met Frederick, sent floral tributes.

Ecclesbourne Coastguard Station was one of the 128 which were closed across Britain between 1905 and 1909. The last men left in October 1908 and the buildings were used for other purposes until 1963, when they had to be demolished because natural erosion had caused the cliff edge to move dangerously close.

Reference: *HSLO* 9th July 1904.

1905

HIGH WIRE HORROR

PRIORY MEADOW

At a public meeting in the Havelock Hotel on 9th March 1864, a committee was formed to create a public recreation ground in the centre of the new part of Hastings. Letters were written to the Countess of Waldegrave and Viscountess Holmesdale, asking to lease two acres of their land, known as Priory Meadow. It would cost £500 to drain, level, turf and fence off the site; £130 was collected at the meeting and the rest would be raised by public subscription.

Once opened the ground was used for cricket, archery, football, tennis, athletics, bicycle races, political meetings, exhibitions, military inspections, drills and parades, pageants, fetes, dog shows, fancy dress carnivals, steam organ performances and circuses. Sadly, it never played host to Blondin, the greatest high-wire performer the world had ever seen.

'Blondin' was the stage name of Frenchman Charles Gravelet, who was celebrated worldwide for his art, most especially because he crossed Niagara Falls 300 times. Such was his fame across the globe that, after his death in 1897, the world's best equilibrists began to proclaim themselves 'the New Blondin', 'Blondin the Second', 'the female Blondin' or 'the American Blondin'. One of them, Will H. Davison, performed in Hastings in 1905.

Born in Ohio in 1860, Davison had toured the USA since he was eighteen, performing at heights of up to 300ft, always without a safety net. His most daring stunt was a wire-walk from Cliff House to Seal Rocks in San Francisco with his younger brother Alex strapped to his back. Their pay for this was a staggering £100 a day (about £46,000 today). In 1894, blindfolded and standing on his head on a wire, he lost his balance and fell 40ft. Although the press predicted he would die, he recovered and returned to his profession.

Having gained fame across North America, it was time for Davison to conquer Britain. In 1900, shortly after turning forty, he accepted a booking to perform for eight weeks in the main transept of London's magnificent Crystal Palace, at a height of 60ft on a wire 5/8ths of an inch thick. The *Daily Telegraph* stated that he exceeded Blondin's greatest triumphs, the highest accolade that any wire-walker could receive. Davison decided to remain in England, calling himself 'Professor' Davison. Successful show contractors Forrest & Beach, seeing his adverts in *The Era*, booked him for a few odd dates, and then in April 1905 invited him to join a five-month tour of Britain, in which he would be the chief attraction, at a salary of £5 10s a week (about £2,000 today).

Sketch of Davison, from an advert for Bile Beans.

Queen's Road, 1905. The Bedford Hotel is out of shot on the right. People lined the streets when travelling shows and fairs arrived in town.

Will's brother, 'Prince' Alexander, standing on his head forty feet above Priory Meadow in August 1905.

On Saturday 10th June Forrest & Beach's Carnival and Old English Fair arrived in Hastings. It would open on Whit Monday, allowing two days to set up the many rides, tents, booths and sideshows. The most time-consuming task was assembling the steam galloper: a showy, noisy, gaudily-painted carousel, upon which the public sat three-abreast on models of horses rotating, rising and falling in the harsh blaze of a hundred electric light bulbs whilst 'Down at the Old Bull and Bush' and other Victorian music hall favourites blared out from the integral barrel organ. The sideshows included shooting galleries and booths where the public paid a fee to throw coconuts, balls or rings at various targets in the hope of winning a cheap trinket. Barkers mingled with the crowds, alternating between tooting on a cornet and announcing that, for tuppence, they could enter any side tent, including one in which lady boxers gave exhibitions of female pugilism.

Although Will Davison was the star of the show the public paid nothing to see him. Being outdoors and high up, he could be seen from outside the enclosure, anyway. His act played a vital promotional role: people could spot him from a distance and would come closer to get a good look at his amazing skills on the wire, then hung around and spent money on the other attractions. Therefore the high wire was always erected first. Davison, who owned and set up his own equipment, strung his wire between two tall poles, 60ft apart, running north to south across Priory Meadow. At 4pm he would give his first performance in the air whilst the steam gallopers, tents and booths were erected on the ground.

On Saturday 10th June Hastings teemed with thousands of townsfolk and summer visitors. Hundreds crowded into Priory Meadow; most came to watch a cricket match, but some were fascinated by the unusual sight of fairground workers setting up the curious and colourful rides and tents. From mid-afternoon people began to arrive to see 'the American Blondin', whom the *Bexhill Observer* called a 'daring and foolish individual' who 'risks his neck twice a day to make the public flesh creep'.

There was a strong cross-wind as Davison ascended the ladder, wearing a pair of velvet shorts fringed with brocade tassels — a design detail repeated on his epaulettes — and clutching a 15ft balancing pole in one hand. Spectators stood still and fell silent as they marvelled at his thrilling routine. About seven minutes into the act, at the Queen's Road end of the high-wire, Davison laid on his back on the wire, raised his knees and placed the pole across them. As he began to stand up from this position the pole slipped and, in trying to grab it, he lost his balance and rolled off the wire, but luckily he managed to catch hold of it with one hand. The audience held its breath as he dangled for a few seconds, gasped as he lost his grip, and some screamed in horror as he plummeted 40ft, hitting the ground head first with a sickening thud.

Bystanders stared in horror as his body writhed in spasms for half a minute, then fell still. Children sobbed as shocked parents led them away.

Police surgeon George Locke had been walking past the Bedford Hotel toward his surgery when his attention was drawn to the strange sight of a figure walking on a wire high up in the air. He chuckled when the man stumbled, thinking it a comical part of the act but, seeing the figure drop, and hearing the horrified shrieks of the spectators, he rushed to the nearest policeman, who conducted him swiftly through the crowds. It was too late: Davison was dead.

At the inquest, held by Charles Davenport Jones at the Market Hall on Tuesday 13th June, Henry Forrest explained that Davison refused a safety net, as it would 'take the novelty off his performance'. The high wind was not to blame for the accident: he had frequently performed in windy conditions, and even during 'thunder and lightning and hail and rain'. The coroner made his disapproval clear, remarking that, so long as people continued to attend, fair organisers would 'pander to the public taste'. Lying down on a thin rope, 40ft in the air was, he asserted, 'outrageously dangerous', and amounted to 'madness'.

Dr Locke's post mortem revealed traces of past illnesses and he suggested that Davison's balance might have been disturbed by 'excitement affecting the brain, from a cold on the old pleurisy, unsteadiness of the heart, or indigestion'. The cause of death was fracture of the ligament which held the spinal cord in place. The jury returned a verdict of 'accidental death'.

The editor of the *HSLO* placed the blame firmly on the spectators: the man had died because he was 'pandering to the tastes of the sensation-loving public'. He then, rather hypocritically, took umbrage at the 'gratuitous insult' levelled at locals by the *Daily News*, which asserted that Davison had 'risked his life and lost it before hundreds of human beings who were paying him to do so'. The *HSLO* retorted that most people present had come to watch a cricket match; besides which, the high-wire act was a free performance.

Priory Meadow and Queen's Road, showing the Bedford Hotel on the corner of Portland Place. Santander currently occupies the site.

The town clerk had received complaints from councillors and ratepayers demanding to know why a dangerous act had been permitted on municipal property. It transpired that neither the county council, the town council nor the police had jurisdiction over circus acts. The only body with the power to impose rules was the Cricket Ground Committee, which could, if it wished, make a proviso that nothing dangerous must take place.

A correspondent to the *HSLO* argued that if the committee intended to ban 'dangerous performances' it could start with cricket and football, which had killed more people 'than all the high rope, trapeze, and wild animal performances put together'. A Sussex cricket umpire had recently been killed by a blow from a ball, yet no ban was so much as mentioned, let alone introduced. Furthermore, wire-walking was not as hazardous as 'the work undertaken daily on scaffolds and high ladders by workmen for a paltry wage'. Another reader pointed out that Davison was the first wire-walker in fifty years to fall to his death.

According to the hackneyed adage 'the show must go on', and the fair opened on Whit Monday as scheduled. Although it rained all day thousands attended and 'the suspended rope from which poor Davison fell was an object of curiosity'. Between the inquest on Tuesday and the funeral on Thursday, Davison was put on display in a handsome and costly open casket, within a sideshow tent (for which there was no entry fee). Hundreds of locals and holidaymakers filed past to pay their respects as floral tributes piled up on the grass outside.

Davison's funeral was paid for by Messrs. Forrest & Beach, who knew how to put on a good show. As the Union Jack was raised to half mast, a huge crowd assembled to watch the cortège leave. Through the glass sides of a magnificent, horse-drawn hearse, hundreds lining the route saw Davison's expensive, polished oak coffin, and the many costly wreaths. The cortège processed slowly through the town to the Borough Cemetery, men removed their hats and everyone bowed their heads. A large group stood solemnly at the graveside as Davison was interred.

The Carnival and Old English Fair completed its week at Hastings and moved on, returning two weeks later for another five-day run. On opening night, a thousand people assembled on Priory Meadow where, at 10pm, a searchlight was thrown dramatically onto a high-wire fifty feet above their heads. A man in a gorgeous velvet tasselled leotard climbed onto a trapeze, from where he addressed the audience. His name, he announced in a grandly theatrical fashion, was Prince Alexander, one of the 'world-famous Davison Brothers of Ohio'. In a routine borrowed from his late brother, who had copied it from Blondin — and without a safety net — he walked along the wire, performed a short sprint, laid down, stood on his head, and finally sat on a chair with two of its legs balancing on the wire. He then took a gracious bow, thanked his enthralled audience and descended, 'amid loud applause and repeated cheering'. Later in the year Alex was engaged to perform daily for three months at the World's Fair in Islington, where he was billed as 'Blondin the Second'.

Over the years, Davison and his gruesome death faded from the memories of locals, even those who witnessed it. In 1944 a correspondent to the *HSLO* asked if anyone could verify that the world's greatest wire-walker, Blondin, died in Hastings, a claim made by A.P. Woods in his 1942 book *I Guarded the Waterfront*. One reader had a vivid memory of seeing a man fall to his death about 1906, but whether it was Blondin, he could not say; another thought the man was 'Blondin the Second'.

Close-up of Alexander performing above Priory Meadow in 1905.

Epilogue: Blondin's son and Hastings

Intrigued by a claim that Blondin 'had relations in Hastings', I set out to prove or disprove it, and found that it was true. After his death his son and assistant, Henry Gravelet, lived here for about eight years. As a child Henry used to be strapped to his father's back as he walked the wire; later he learned to set up and test the equipment, then trained as a pyrotechnist in order to produce spectacular firework displays to enhance his father's thrilling performances.

At the age of seventy-two, Blondin married his second wife, a twenty-nine-year-old barmaid. When he died two years later, in 1897, Henry left his wife and seven children to live in Hastings with his widowed stepmother. He passed her off as his wife — an easy lie, since she was already Mrs Gravelet! Being a primo of the Royal Antediluvian Order of Buffaloes, he soon obtained the references necessary to become the licensee of the Bedford Hotel on Queen's Road. He traded shamelessly on his famous father's stage name, using it in adverts, and sometimes called himself 'Mr Blondin'.

The 1901 census shows him living at the Bedford Hotel with his mistress Katherine, her five-year-old illegitimate daughter, Kate, and his widowed sister, Adèle. A few weeks later Katherine died of cancer and was buried in Blondin's elaborate grave. Henry gave up the pub and by 1911 had returned to his wife and children in London. The electoral register for 1905 to 1907 shows 'Henry Gravelet Blondin' renting a furnished room on the top floor of 117 Queen's Road, opposite Waterworks Road, so he may have been in Hastings on the day 'the American Blondin' died on Priory Meadow in 1905.

	Henry Gravelet	Head	m	40	Publican
	Katherine do	Wife	m	38	
	Adele Parton	Sister	Wid	44	Living on own means
	Kate James	Niece		5	

References: *The Era* 15th April 1893 & 18th May 1901; *Daily Telegraph* 27th October 1900; *Bexhill Observer* 1st July 1905. *HSLO* 17th & 24th June 1905; 5th August 1905; 3rd, 17th & 24th June 1944.

1910

THE INFIRMARY ENIGMA

FREDERICK ROAD

For many years each parish in England had its own small poorhouse or workhouse, but in 1834 they grouped into unions to build and share the cost of one large establishment. The fourteen parishes in the Hastings Union constructed theirs in Cackle Street, Ore. When it opened in 1837, it was the largest building in Hastings. From 1900 new buildings were added on the other side of the road and the original workhouse became an infirmary.

In the boardroom of the workhouse on 20th December 1910, an inquest was held by Coroner William Glenister. An elderly infirmary patient, John James Byron Mcconnochie, had shot himself. Admitted in March 1910 suffering from severe bronchitis, John was 'bedridden to a certain extent, but had the use of his hands'. The jury returned a verdict of suicide but had no idea how he had acquired and secreted a gun.

About midnight on 14th December a nurse gave John some hot milk to help him sleep. At 4.45am she and others heard a loud bang. Wardsman Colborn took it for the crack of a horse-whip; Philip Down, a patient, assumed a stone had exploded in the fireplace. An hour later Colborn noticed blood on John's sheet and called the nurses. Pulling back his bedclothes they found a revolver grasped in John's right hand, powder marks around his mouth, and blood and gore everywhere. A notebook found on a nearby window sill contained his last words:

> Good-bye. I leave the place where man has no pity for the suffering. Away to God. Who has forgiveness and mercy unfathomable. I am entirely justified in my act, for I only know my weary suffering, remembering there are no limits to indictments which can be preferred against a dead man.

The nurses were baffled. It was impossible to bring a revolver into the ward. There was nowhere that one could be secreted without a member of staff finding it. When admitted John's clothes were searched and taken away, his standard-issue pyjamas were removed every day for ablutions, and his bed was re-made daily. Each inmate was allocated a small bedside locker, which was frequently emptied to be scrubbed out. Every parcel brought in by a visitor was opened and the contents approved (or not) by the matron. In any case, John had never received a parcel, nor had a visitor for many months.

The infirmary was on the east side of Frederick Road. In 1930 the workhouse became the Municipal Hospital, and was renamed St Helens Hospital in 1948 and closed in 1998. It was replaced by the Conquest in 1998. The infirmary is among the old workhouse buildings which have been converted into dwellings.

Illustrated Police News artist's impression of the scene.

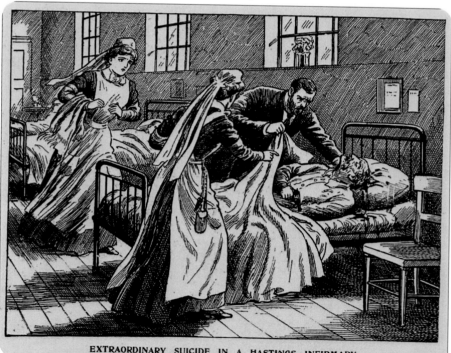

EXTRAORDINARY SUICIDE IN A HASTINGS INFIRMARY.

Born in 1839, John was a Scotsman and the son of an army captain. Although in business as a tailor, he had committed a robbery in 1863 and served a year in prison. He then turned his whole life around: by 1903 he held a respected post as a council vaccination officer, was married, and had two fine sons. He retired on a pension in 1904, but in 1905, devastated by the death of his wife, he attempted suicide by drinking poison. After he recovered he took a trip to South Africa, and on his return settled in Hastings, lodging at St Mary's Terrace and later at 14 Mann Street.

Telegraphist Alfred Mcconnochie travelled from London for the inquest. He deposed that his father was a 'repulsive' man of 'excitable temperament' who was 'somewhat addicted to intemperance' (in other words, an alcoholic). The last time they met, back in 1907, Alfred confiscated a revolver from his father because he had threatened suicide. It was still in his possession.

The riddle was partly solved by a charwoman and a publican. When Harry Johnson was landlord of the Angel Inn, St Mary's Terrace, John asked him to look

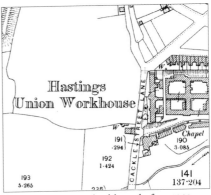

The workhouse buildings before 1903.

after a sealed parcel. When Johnson was packing up to move to Tonbridge, he had no idea where John was, so he opened it. Inside was a loaded revolver. He re-sealed it and took it to his new pub, knowing John would be directed there if he came asking for him. Two years later the publican received a redirected letter from John, asking him to post the parcel. But Johnson would not put a loaded gun in the Royal Mail. After another letter, threatening legal action, Johnson asked a policeman to unload it, then sent it, unloaded but with the bullets enclosed, to an address in Hastings.

Mrs Down's husband occupied the bed next to John and she would post letters for the old man. At the end of July she took a letter for Mr Johnson to the Angel and was given his new address. John wrote a fresh letter, which Mrs Down posted. At the end of August, John gave her a parcel, saying a carrier would call at her house for it. However, several weeks later, none had called, so she gave it back to him in September.

Police and infirmary staff found out how John had obtained the gun, but they never discovered where he secreted it for three months without it being found by the staff.

London Daily News 17th August 1903; *HSLO* 17th & 24th December 1910.

Mr F.W. Womersley, from a group photo of the chess club committee.

One Revolver; Two Dead

Cambridge Road & Station Road

Frederick Womersley's father, Charles, was known as the 'Grand Old Man of Hastings', not just because he lived to the age of ninety but because he was so well known about town, having been variously an upholsterer, undertaker, furniture dealer and auctioneer, an outspoken Radical Dissenter and a Wesleyan preacher. Frederick, the fourth of his eight children, was born in Hastings in 1839. At age nineteen he made his sweetheart pregnant and baby Emily was born just weeks after their marriage. This slight indiscretion was soon forgotten as the couple went on to have five more children and to lead 'blameless lives'.

Frederick was best known for co-founding the Hastings & St Leonards Chess Club in 1882, at a meeting of nine like-minded gentlemen in the Temperance Hotel, Queen's Road. Whilst serving on its committee for over a quarter of a century he frequented tournaments at Simpson's and other London venues, joined club tours to Scotland and Ireland and competed in first-class matches and tournaments. He won many prizes, including the club championship five times. As the club gained worldwide repute, he was elected its vice-president. In 1895 he helped organise the Hastings International Tournament, remembered as one of the greatest in chess history. Frederick also wrote a popular chess column in the *HSLO*, which was enjoyed by many readers.

Having been apprenticed to his father, Frederick took over his long-established upholstery business at 12 York Buildings (now Wellington Place). In middle age he switched to a new career as an accountant, auctioneer and auditor, and became manager of the Hastings Permanent Building Society. For fifteen years he was based at 5 Trinity Street, which served as office and home. In late 1909 he moved around the corner to a former lodging house situated in a more prominent location, on the main road and tram route to Silverhill. It had four storeys, six bedrooms and three receptions. The whole of the ground floor was earmarked for business, with the front parlour turned into an office. In the basement was a kitchen leading to a small outdoor area under the front office window. By then his wife, youngest daughter and one son had died and his other sons had left home, so only he and Emily moved into 56 Cambridge Road.

Father and daughter were among the most recognisable and well-liked residents of Hastings, each having gained renown in their own right. As she approached fifty Emily was well known locally for performing piano recitals and conducting orchestral concerts, and as a private music tutor for decades, she had taught hundreds of pupils. She was also esteemed for her charitable

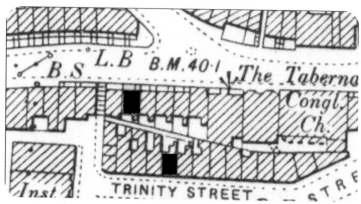

Map with 5 Trinity Street and 56 Cambridge Road marked in black.

1909 advert and notice of change of address.

The Hastings and East Sussex Permanent Benefit
BUILDING SOCIETY

HAS REMOVED THE OFFICE TO

No. 56, CAMBRIDGE RD., HASTINGS

FOR THE THRIFTY.—Small monthly payments, to which compound interest is added, soon realise a little capital.

FOR THE INVESTOR.—Deposits of £5 and upwards are received, on which interest is paid half-yearly. The deposits can be withdrawn at one month's notice.

FOR THE BORROWER.—Advances made on Freehold and Leasehold Properties, repayable by monthly instalments covering principal and interest; the interest charged is only one penny per pound per month on the balance due to the Society.

NO LAW COSTS.

All information of the Manager—

F. W. WOMERSLEY,

56, CAMBRIDGE ROAD.

and religious work. As well as being a prominent name in the world of chess, Frederick had earned a reputation as a fair and trustworthy businessman, and for holding various honorary positions. He was also respected for his religious activities connected with the Croft Congregational Chapel and its Sunday School. At seventy-two he was still putting in a hard day's work at the office whilst Emily divided her time between the world of music and keeping house.

❋ ❋ ❋

Born near Redruth, Cornwall, in 1859, Joseph James, known as JJ, was a son of Captain A.T. James, a prominent manager and broker in the tin-mine industry, whose other sons founded the firm of James Brothers, consulting engineers to the gold mining industry worldwide. They made a great deal of money and lived in smart houses in wealthy areas of London and Surrey. JJ was the maverick: he studied pharmacology and dentistry, which were, unfortunately, less lucrative.

At twenty-one JJ married a book-keeper and within a few years they had a houseful of children. To increase his income he indulged in a certain amount of self-aggrandisement, advertising as 'Dr Joseph James, the Eminent London Dentist' or 'J. James D.D.S., R.D.S., doctor of dental surgery'. A neighbour described him as 'eccentric' because he jeopardised his thriving business by posting 'peculiar notices', such as 'All work and no play makes Jack a dull boy, I am off for four days' holiday'.

After Harriet died in 1895, leaving JJ with six children aged between three and fourteen, he married his sister-in-law Eleanor, and his children's aunt became their stepmother. The union was invalid because until 1907 it was illegal to marry a deceased wife's sister. Five more children came along, and life became a struggle. At times JJ went off the rails. In 1905, when he had a dental surgery and chemist shop, he was arrested for illegally dispensing chloroform; luckily, he was acquitted. He would walk about with a loaded revolver, and fire it to threaten people who annoyed him, though he was careful never to shoot anyone, and so avoided prosecution.

About 1908 he developed heart and lung trouble. Hoping sea air would cure him, the family moved to Hastings, renting a nine-roomed maisonette within a substantial house at 38 Nelson Road. He turned the ground floor front parlour into a pharmacy, and his children would deliver to customers. Business was slow, and within two years the stress and worry of trying to support seven people on a pittance had driven JJ almost to the brink of a nervous breakdown. In desperation, he wrote to the superintendent of the Royal Holloway Sanatorium:

> I am a chemist and have been in business for 35 years. I have had to provide for a large family and have had to work very hard. Some time ago I had a severe reverse, so that I at times become temporarily insane, and unaccountable for my actions.

56 Cambridge Road in 2019. In 1931 it was renumbered to 39. Frederick's office is now a flat. The railings are new because the rooflight for the area yard has only just been reopened.

Looking east down Cambridge Road toward the Memorial in the 1870s. No.56 is just out of shot on the far right.

He needed 'a few weeks quiet rest' and, in lieu of payment, offered his professional services as a pharmacist during his stay. Despite saying that his doctor and a local JP would provide character references, his offer was rejected. As he could not afford the fees, JJ did not get the rest and treatment he urgently needed.

In the summer of 1910 JJ tried to raise cash by selling his photographic dark slides. A buyer offered him a revolver as payment. JJ had given his own gun to his son to take to Canada, so he accepted it, saying it would do for his other son, who was also emigrating there. However, by 1911 it was still in his possession.

The stress and strain on JJ is evident from the mistakes he made on his 1911 census return. He initially included his eldest daughter, momentarily forgetting she had left home in 1903; and in a column reserved for blindness, deafness and mental illness he listed his bronchitis and heart trouble.

By the spring of 1911 JJ's rent arrears stood at £28. Mr Womersley, who handled the letting, sent bailiff Joseph Collins to 38 Nelson Road with a warrant of distress. He gained entry to the basement and remained there, 'in possession'. JJ brandished a revolver and fired a shot into the fire-grate as a warning of 'how he would serve them' if they dared take his furniture. He threatened the petrified bailiff: 'You had best clear out, as in the state of my head at present I shall not be answerable for my actions'. He then pointed the revolver directly at Collins, who pleaded: 'For God's sake, put that down! You have a wife and family, and so do I!' JJ replied: 'If I wanted to do away with you I have plenty of poison upstairs!' Collins fled in terror and refused ever to go back.

Despite his bluster, JJ knew his goods had to be sold. When auctioneer William Neeves Oldham visited, JJ said he had seventy new cameras (his commercial stock) and a wealthy brother who 'had promised to meet any deficiency'. He offered for auction fifteen cameras and some furniture. Mr Oldham warned that if they failed to raise £28, he would send another bailiff. JJ warned: 'If you do, he will have a rough time of it'.

JJ felt so ashamed of his plight that he requested his goods be removed after dark, hoping the neighbours would not see. Too embarrassed to show his face at the auction, he sent his daughters May, aged fifteen, and Gladys, thirteen. They noted the price fetched by each item, added it up, then went home to break the bad news that the total raised was only £14 12s. JJ had expected double that and wanted to have a word with Mr Womersley. Gladys donned a navy blue tam-o'-shanter, JJ pocketed a loaded revolver, and together they set out for 56 Cambridge Road.

It was a warm, sunny afternoon. Emily Womersley sat outside in the basement area, brushing her cat; her father was above her, working at his desk in the front office. When JJ and Gladys arrived at about 4.45pm the front door was open, but the inner lobby door was locked. JJ pulled the bell and Frederick let them in. He ushered JJ into his office whilst Gladys waited by the front door.

Joseph James.

She heard her father remonstrating angrily about the low prices accepted for his cameras, demanding to know 'how an eight-guinea Warwick machine should go for eight shillings'. When JJ asked if any more of his goods would have to be sold, Frederick prevaricated. Gladys heard the words, 'Oh, Mr James!' followed by a bang. She opened the front door and ran outside.

Richard Francis, a riding master at Dick Russell's in Royal Mews (now 4 Cambridge Gardens), heard shouting then a gunshot. He crossed the road and, as he entered no.56, a second shot rang out. Through an open door he saw a man holding a revolver and saying: 'You have asked for this' to an elderly, bearded gent lying on the floor, his head covered with blood.

JJ told Francis it was an accident and he would give himself up to a policeman. Francis went outside, where a few people had gathered, and shouted 'Police'. A passing milkman hurried to the Albert Memorial and brought back PC John Lawrence on a tramcar. Mr Francis went next door to Dr Field, who happened to be the police surgeon.[1]

Down in the basement, Emily heard neither doorbell nor quarrel, only two loud explosions, as though the tyres of two motor-cars had burst. Hearing someone shout 'Oh, you murderer', she went upstairs to find strangers in the front hall and a crowd outside. She tried to enter her father's office but PC Lawrence redirected her into a back room, told her to wait there, and closed the door.

Meanwhile JJ was explaining, 'I shot him. I am very, very sorry'. Seeing Lawrence he added: 'Constable, there has been an accident with a revolver and I wish to give myself up'. Lawrence retorted that one shot from a gun could be accidental, but not two, half a minute apart. He demanded the revolver, but JJ seated himself in Frederick's revolving leather chair and replied, 'We will see about that at the station'. Dr Field arrived and JJ was again asked for the gun. Eventually he handed it over, remarking, in a blasé fashion, that he 'always carried one'. Dr Field examined it briefly, then turned his attention to the victim. He deduced that, after being shot in the buttock, Frederick had crawled under the table, where he received a fatal bullet in the head. Field offered to break the awful news to his neighbour, Emily, who was still confined in the back room, frantic with worry.

Detective Sub-Inspector Edward Orlando Chantler arrived. Born in Kent in November 1875, he had joined Hastings police at nineteen, living in the section house above the police station at 95 Bohemia Road. After his mother died his father and siblings moved to Hastings. By 1911 all five were living at 26 Mann Street, and his younger brother had also joined the force.

Edward Chantler had given the force sixteen years of truly excellent service, receiving a shower of accolades. He had been formally commended twelve times and rewarded by the Watch Committee four times. Progression had

1. Adolphus Theodore Field LSA (1861–1936). Police surgeon for Hastings for 30 years, during which time he performed 2,250 post mortems. He was replaced by Dr Nesbitt Wood (see page 176).

DISTRESSING FATALITY AT HASTINGS.
CHEMIST CHARGED WITH MURDERING A MANAGER.

An artist's impression of the shooting, published in the *Illustrated Police News* on 23rd September 1911. Note how he cleverly hid the gunman's face, because he did not know what JJ looked like.

been swift: by age twenty-five he was a detective and only a fortnight previously had been promoted to sub-inspector by the chief constable, who described him as 'a most able, conscientious detective officer, discreet in his enquiries, and a man to be thoroughly relied upon'. Chantler's future, he added, 'was a very bright one indeed'. At only thirty-five Chantler was in charge of the detective department and on track to be a future chief constable.

Chantler examined the revolver. Of the five chambers, three held bullets. He placed it in his right-hand jacket pocket and cautioned JJ, 'Whatever you say now may be taken down in writing and used as evidence against you'. JJ explained, 'We had a quarrel and I fired a shot to frighten him. But he knocked my hand up. It was an accident. I am quite willing to go with you'. In view of this Chantler saw no need to handcuff him for the short walk to the police station. Gladys, still waiting outside, followed along behind, stood outside the station awhile, hoping her father would emerge, then went home and told her mother everything. After a while PC George Milton turned up, demanding to search the house.

A crowd of locals loitered outside no.56 for hours, shocked and puzzled at the senseless murder of a well known, mild-mannered, benevolent and deeply religious elderly gent. A local photographer arrived to record the awful scene for the police, then Frederick's corpse was covered up discreetly and quietly removed to the mortuary.

The funeral, held at Robertson Street Congregational Church on 18th September, was well attended by Mr Womersley's many business, church and municipal associates. Among the floral tributes was one from the chess club, which had voted to send a wreath 'costing not more than one guinea' (about £100 today). He was laid to rest in the Borough Cemetery.

The case against JJ was heard at Hastings Police Court over three sessions (14th, 21st and 23rd September). Wearing a loose lounge suit and pince-nez spectacles, JJ was formally charged with 'feloniously killing and slaying' Frederick Womersley. When invited to question the witnesses, JJ's former apologetic tone had vanished. His demeanour was argumentative, and he grasped the opportunity to cross-examine with considerable relish. He began by labelling the evidence of Richard Francis 'a tissue of falsehoods' and challenged every point he had given in evidence.

JJ: Did you hear me call 'Police, help, and doctor'?
Francis: No, you did not.
JJ: It is merely a case of one man contradicting another.

JJ: You say three or four shots were fired. Are you aware only two shots had been fired? If all your evidence is taken on that scale, it is not worth much.
Francis: I said I thought I heard two or three; I could not say for certain.
JJ: I don't think it is any good going into the matter. Your evidence is not satisfactory.

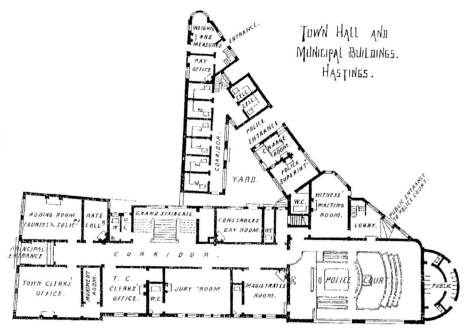

Plan of the ground floor of the Town Hall showing the police station on the north-east side and the police court in the right corner. From *The Builder*, 1881.

Hastings Town Hall in 1900. The walls and gates have gone but the turret survives and is now a fast food outlet.

JJ: In which pocket do you say I put the revolver?
Francis: Right-hand.
JJ: You said right-hand jacket. I have not got one. It was the trousers.

JJ: In what direction was the man's face turned, right or left?
Francis: Left.
JJ: Facing the fireplace or door?
Francis: I can't say.
JJ: Your evidence is not worth taking down.

When DSI Chantler made his deposition JJ attempted to bamboozle him:

JJ: Where is the detective with whom I walked down Cambridge Road to the police station?
Chantler: I was the officer.
JJ: He was shorter than you?
Chantler: No; I went with you myself.

JJ then asserted that Chantler had allowed him to retain possession of the revolver until they reached the police station. This was as outrageous as it was unexpected. Chantler would never have allowed such a thing, but he suddenly realised that he could not disprove it. At the front desk, Warren had witnessed the revolver emerging from Chantler's pocket, but that was *after* they arrived at the station. When Chantler told JJ he was wrong, he retorted: 'I say the same to you', and when JJ concluded: 'It is no good going further; it is only a waste of time. My word is as good as yours,' Chantler replied: 'Yes, quite.' A firm denial was needed, but instead Chantler had unwittingly conceded that the word of a murder suspect was equal to that of a police sub-inspector.

JJ's wicked claim served a dual purpose. It would help convince the magistrates that, on the day, Chantler believed the shooting was an accident, but it also called his judgement into question. JJ's apologetic manner, and his willingness to accompany him to the station, had lulled Chantler into thinking there was no need to handcuff him, nor for another officer to walk with them. Clearly, it did not occur to him that JJ would dispute any aspect of his arrest. He must have felt foolish for failing to cover his own back.

As Chantler left for work on Wednesday 20th September his sister asked if he would be returning home for lunch. He replied, 'No, I feel sure I shalln't today'. The inquest into Mr Womersley's death was scheduled for that afternoon and he needed to prepare his deposition. Mindful that JJ was claiming otherwise, Chantler needed to make sure his statement was emphatic on the subject of who had possession of the gun en route to the station.

Arriving at work at 8.15am, he called out to Sgt Mellor to book him on duty, then busied himself in his office for fifteen minutes. He took JJ's revolver and bullets from his desk drawer, asked Mellor, who was gaoler, for the bunch of keys to the cells, and let himself into the one they used to store exhibits.

Just after 9am Mellor, needing the cell keys, went to find Chantler. To his horror he found him slumped on the bench, blood and gore spattered on the walls behind his head. JJ's revolver was in his hand, yet Mellor had heard no gunshot. He summoned SI Warren, who was Chantler's closest friend. Though shocked to his core, he kept his nerve, did his duty and coolly examined the scene. The revolver was empty when Chantler locked it in his office drawer. Now, two chambers were loaded and one contained an empty cartridge. Dr Field was summoned, and confirmed that Chantler had deliberately placed the gun in his mouth and pulled the trigger.

The inquest on Mr Womersley resumed that afternoon. A large group of excited locals collected outside the town hall, and as soon as the doors opened every seat was filled. Depositions were given by Emily Womersley, PC Lawrence and Mr Francis, and after four hours the proceedings were again adjourned.

By the time of JJ's second police court hearing, on 21st September, most of the town knew of Chantler's suicide and a huge crowd assembled outside, eager to secure the best seats. Within minutes of the doors opening there was standing room only, and the court was 'crowded to suffocation'. Several local dignitaries attended, as well as Mr Coulson Kernahan, a writer of detective, crime and fantasy novels.[1] Also present was Chief Constable Frederick James, who not only shared a surname with the accused, but also hailed from Cornwall and may have been a distant relation.

The defence team comprised barrister Mr Baker, solicitor Mr A.M. Elliott, and, surprisingly, Richard David Muir, a distinguished, prominent and successful barrister who rarely acted for the defence. He had been senior counsel to the Treasury at the Old Bailey for a decade, a Bencher of the Middle Temple for two years, and had recently shot to fame owing to his successful prosecution of Dr Crippen in late 1910. Muir's fees were astronomical; doubtless he was engaged by JJ's wealthy brothers.

Joseph James walked slowly into the dock, head held high, pince-nez almost on the tip of his nose, and bowed slightly to the magistrates. He showed great composure, and before being told to sit down placed both hands over the edge of the dock and glanced calmly round the court.

The prosecution's case was opened by Mr W.J. Day, a Treasury solicitor. He argued that the shooting was an act of revenge for the low prices accepted for the auctioned goods. JJ had deliberately taken a loaded revolver when he set out. Had the shooting been accidental, the bullets would have been fired in quick succession, whereas the gap between the two shots was sufficient to allow Mr Francis to cross a wide road.

Various witnesses gave evidence, then came the highlight of the day: JJ's thirteen-year-old daughter was to be questioned. There was a great deal of shuffling and whispering at the back of the court from people trying to catch

1. John Coulson Kernahan (1858–1943) had moved to Hastings in 1907 and lived at 25 Collier Road.

The Guardian 21st and 22nd September 1911.

HASTINGS MURDER CASE.

DETECTIVE INSPECTOR FOUND DEAD IN THE CELLS.

Detective Inspector Chantler, who had charge of the Hastings murder case, was found dead yesterday morning in the cells department of the Town Hall at Hastings.

The murder case is that in which Mr. Womersley, an accountant and the manager of a building society, was found shot dead in his office, and standing in the room was a local chemist holding a revolver. This revolver was found by Inspector Chantler's body.

The inquest on Mr. Womersley was resumed yesterday and again adjourned. The evidence of Detective Chantler was read over, and the coroner referred to Chantler's death as a very painful incident. Chantler, he said, always enjoyed the confidence of his superiors.

HASTINGS MURDER CASE.

A POLICE INSPECTOR'S SUICIDE.

An inquest was held at Hastings last night on Inspector Chantler, who was found shot at the police station on Wednesday, and a verdict of suicide during temporary insanity was returned. The inspector was engaged on the Womersley murder case, and it was stated that on arriving at the police station on Wednesday he took the keys and went to the cell where the exhibits, including a revolver, were kept in a case. No report was heard, but about an hour later he was found shot with a revolver grasped in his right hand.

The Chief Constable spoke highly of Chantler's ability, and said that he had admitted making a slight mistake in his evidence at the inquest on Mr. Womersley, but it was not material, and need not have worried him.

a glimpse of Gladys James in her navy blue tam-o'-shanter. When she took the stand JJ became agitated and stared at the floor. Gladys was questioned by Mr Day, who took her through the events of 13th September as she boldly but politely replied 'Yes sir' and 'No sir', as appropriate. She had never seen a revolver in the house and was unaware that her father possessed one. When asked who carried the weapon to the police station, Gladys stated that the butt of the gun was sticking out of her father's left hand trouser pocket.[1]

The hearing was adjourned and that evening an inquest opened to examine Chantler's death. PC Robert Chantler told the coroner that his brother had no personal problems, was not depressed, and was his usual self that morning. Sgt Mellor knew Chantler for sixteen years, professionally and personally, and his suicide was entirely beyond his comprehension. The chief constable, who had known Chantler for five years, was equally baffled. He said the detective had admitted to making 'a slight mistake' at the first session of Mr Womersley's inquest, but it was not material to the case and nothing to worry about.

The coroner asked Dr Field if handling a murder case could 'cause depression to a sensitive man' or if being in a cell with 'gruesome exhibits' could bring on 'an attack of impulsive insanity'. Dr Field knew Chantler well and did not think such things were sufficient to induce him to take his life.

After two hours of evidence the coroner said he had rarely addressed a jury under sadder circumstances. An acquaintance of Chantler's for sixteen years, he agreed that he was 'the very last man' to be 'the author of his own death' and yet no other explanation fitted the facts. The jury returned a verdict of 'suicide during temporary insanity'.

1. JJ's descendants believe that Gladys had been primed to lie.

On 23rd September the court was again crowded for the resumed hearing into the shooting of Mr Womersley. After waiting placidly through three hours of evidence, 'unmoved throughout Mr Muir's examination', JJ 'displayed eagerness to tell his tale'. He stood 'erect in the dock ... his eagerness vanished, he was the cool, collected individual once more'. Speaking quietly, he explained how Mr Womersley had shot himself.

I wish to explain why I fired the revolver. On Wednesday, 13 September, in the afternoon, I called on Mr Womersley for a business chat. Our chat over, I gave him notice that I should damage his mantelpiece. It would be a means for my getting a summons for damages in the County Court, and so air there some of the grievances which I had. Accordingly, I rose from my chair — I was then seated at the end of the table near the window on the door side — drew the revolver from my right-hand pocket, and pointed at the jamb of the mantelpiece opposite my right hand. The muzzle was slightly depressed, and would have hit a spot about 18 inches from the shelf of the mantel. I glanced at the weapon to see that it was in order, but on looking up found that Mr Womersley was sliding from his chair, head to the window, face downwards. I at once saw that his head was in the line of fire; my finger was on the trigger, I had brought slight pressure to bear, and anxious not to hit him, like a flash I altered the direction of the revolver to the other jamb. I had not time to notice that the muzzle had been acutely depressed. The explosion took place, and Womersley was hit on the right haunch.

I was horrified and dazed, and for a moment did not know what to do. I thought we must have help, and went towards the door. The door was then about 18 inches open. Just as I was about to open it further, I heard a noise at my back, and wheeling round to the left I saw that Womersley had risen from under the table about 18 inches from the end.

The expression on that man's face I shall never forget. Fiendish rage and hatred! I felt positively afraid of him. Glaring at the revolver which was in my right hand instinctively made me remove my finger from the trigger catch, and with it and the rest of my hand firmly grasped the stock of the revolver. We were then about three paces apart. He lunged towards me, and I put up my left arm to fend him off. With his right hand he broke down my defence, and with his left knocked up my right hand which held the revolver shoulder high, with his right hand he grasped the muzzle of the revolver; with his left hand he grabbed at the trigger guard. His fingers became entangled with the trigger. Turning his face to the fireplace and slightly inclined to the right, inclining his body also to the window as though as to get the weight of his body as well as his arm force into the coming wrench, he made a terrific wrench. I felt my hold on the stock loosen; there was an explosion, and Womersley fell to the floor shot.

JJ paused awhile, and added, 'That is all'. The magistrates dismissed his tale and committed him to Lewes Assizes 'on the capital charge of wilfully murdering Frederick William Womersley'. JJ said, 'Quite so', and left the dock.

Chantler's funeral, on 25th September. St Andrew's church was packed solid with family, friends and acquaintances, police officers from Hastings, Bexhill and Eastbourne, magistrates, town hall and court staff. He was interred in the Borough Cemetery.

Two days later the inquest on Frederick Womersley resumed. It filled five-and-three-quarter hours. SI Warren deposed that, when Chantler arrived at the station, he produced the revolver from his right-hand jacket pocket. Gladys was called, and 'boldly' answered all questions put to her. The hearing ended with Dr Thomas Redmayne[1] questioning Dr Field. 'The contest between the two doctors', remarked the *HSLO*, 'was the only sparkling moment of a very monotonous afternoon'. Annoyingly, the paper did not reproduce it. The coroner, seeing the clock approach 9pm, adjourned again. The verdict came at the resumed hearing on 4th October. The jury took just seven minutes to reach a verdict of 'wilful murder'.

The coroner expressed deep regret at the untimely death of Mr Womersley, a man 'of the highest integrity' and 'the kindliest disposition'. He concluded: 'All that remains of him now is his name as an upright, honourable man, who led a blameless life.'

The murder trial began at 11am on Monday 11th December 1911 at the Winter Assizes in Lewes. Counsel for the Director of Public Prosecutions were Mr C.F. Gill KC and Mr Beaumont Morice, whilst for the defence were Mr R.D. Muir and Mr C.F. Baker. The judge was Sir Thomas Scrutton (who later presided over the trial of George Joseph Smith in the infamous 'Brides-in-the-Bath' case). Expecting an open-and-shut case, he asked for another to be lined up for the afternoon sitting.

Before the trial began counsel held a private consultation in the judge's room to discuss whether JJ was in a fit state of mind to plead. Having received 'certain information' the DPP had investigated his mental history. Dr Charles Planck, superintendent of Brighton County Asylum, Dr William Alexander Dow, medical officer of Lewes Prison and Dr Theophilus Bulkeley Hyslop, former superintendent of Bethlem Asylum in London, had examined JJ and declared him to be 'of unsound mind'. Their conclusion was supported by Thurstan Peter, a solicitor from Redruth with considerable knowledge of lunacy, who gave public talks on 'How to deal with the feeble-minded'. He had travelled from Cornwall to save JJ from the hangman's noose.

Peter claimed that madness ran through JJ's veins. His maternal grandfather, Samuel Gray, was a beer retailer, grocer, innkeeper and brewer, but

1. Dr Redmayne (1864–1931) worked in Hastings hospitals for thirty-four years, becoming the senior surgeon. A road has been named in his honour on the former site of the Royal East Sussex Hospital.

all the village knew he was insane; in fact 'as mad as old Gray' was a common expression in the district. Gray's niece was notoriously eccentric: local children were afraid of her and she would deliberately grimace, just to scare them. Gray's son Thomas had committed suicide and his daughter Johanna (JJ's mother) had spent fifteen years in an insane asylum until her death in 1896.

The jury decided that JJ was unfit to plead, and must instead be 'kept in strict custody until His Majesty's pleasure be known'. JJ spent the remainder of his life in Broadmoor Criminal Lunatic Asylum. Being of superior education, he became the institution's librarian, though in later years, suffering failing eyesight, he was a storesman.

His wife Eleanor and the remaining dependent children moved to Reading to be close to JJ and he was permitted to visit them; family photos show him relaxing in the garden. Although deemed sufficiently sane to be repeatedly allowed home for a day, he was considered too mentally ill to be allowed to live there permanently. Eleanor 'appealed tirelessly' for his release, but it was never granted and he died in Broadmoor in 1931, aged seventy-one.

References: *HSLO* 16th, 23rd & 30th September, 7th October, 9th & 16th December 1911; *Cornishman* 14th December 1911; *Illustrated Police News* 23rd and 30th September 1911; *The Observer* 24th September 1911. The story was covered in *The Times* and the *Daily Mail* as well as newspapers across Britain and in several English speaking countries.

JJ and his daughter, Olive.

1920

MURDER ON THE HASTINGS EXPRESS

WHITE ROCK INFIRMARY

On Monday 12th January at 3.20pm a ten-coach London, Brighton & South Coast train left Victoria bound for Sussex. It stopped only at Lewes and Polegate Junction, where it divided. The front six coaches went to Eastbourne and the rear four to Hastings. At Polegate three platelayers entered a third class compartment in the third carriage of the Hastings section. George settled into the far corner, Ernie sat next to him and Bill chose the corner seat diagonally opposite them. It was 5pm and night had fallen. In the dim gas light they noticed a small figure snoozing in the corner opposite George. She had slid down the upholstered bench seat whilst asleep, causing her sealskin coat and her skirt to ride up to her knees. An open book was on her lap but her newspaper had slipped to the floor. During the fifteen-minute run to Bexhill George tried not to stare at a lady whose legs were exposed, but he glanced casually in her direction now and again, and saw her eyes open and close periodically, like someone drifting in and out of sleep. After a while what he thought was a veil over her face began to look more like dried blood. He made a comment to Bill, who gave no reply.

At Bexhill the platelayers got off and George drew Guard Harry Duck's attention to the lady. Duck bent down and peered at her. He saw blood, apparently from a head injury. He decided to take her on to Hastings, which had better first aid facilities and a hospital near the station. His off-duty colleague, Guard George Waters, sat with her during the ten-minute journey. After she was taken off in an ambulance, the carriage was shunted into a siding, where its door was sealed with a label to preserve the scene.

A young house surgeon, Miss Annie Beattie,[1] examined the mystery passenger. She had sustained three heavy blows to the left side of her head, causing a fractured skull and two deep lacerations of the scalp, from which a portion of brain protruded. This was no accident: only a vicious assault could have caused such terrible injuries. As the unconscious woman 'lingered between life and death', the line was searched for a weapon or any other clue. Nothing was found.

Rosa Peal told railway staff that a friend she was meeting off a train had not arrived, and they directed her to the hospital, where she identified

---

1. Born in Ireland in 1894, Dr Beattie qualified in 1918 and came to Hastings, where she remained until her death in 1990. In 1939 she was living and working at 26 Warrior Square Terrace with her three sisters, all of whom were also medical doctors.

A press photograph of a similar train at Lewes, to illustrate how the suspect alighted. Inset: Guard Harry Duck and his walrus moustache. Duck, 52, lived at 142 Railway Cottages, West Marina.

The compartment in which Nurse Shore travelled, photographed in Hastings sidings. The door is labelled to protect the crime scene. *Daily Mirror* 16th & 17th January 1920.

Guard George Waters, 48, who lived at 8 Carisbrooke Road.

Mr. G. Waters

the woman. Her name was Florence Nightingale Shore, so named because her father was a cousin of the famous nurse and heroine of the Crimea, who was her godmother. Miss Shore, who was fifty-five, had been travelling to Warrior Square in order to spend a week with Mrs Peal, her husband and her teenage daughters in their flat above her tea-rooms at 75 Bohemia Road.

Born in 1865, Miss Shore led an extraordinary life for a woman of her era. Spirited and daring, in her mid-twenties she spent two years working in China, a mysterious (some said 'inscrutable') faraway land. After suitable training she embarked on her distinguished career as a military nurse, serving in South Africa during the Boer War, and in Europe during the Great War. Working for the French Red Cross and then Queen Alexandra's Imperial Military Nursing Service, she spent five years nursing war-wounded soldiers in hospitals, casualty clearing stations, advanced dressing stations and ambulance trains. Her bravery was illustrated by her refusal to leave her patients, even when bombs were falling nearby. She was highly esteemed by medical and military colleagues and loved by her grateful patients. French African troops dubbed her 'The White Queen', and an army doctor described her as 'one of the most unselfish and self-sacrificing women I have ever met'. For her years of heroism during history's worst and bloodiest war she was awarded the Royal Red Cross, a military decoration whose first recipient was her famous godmother.

Since being demobilised in December 1919 Miss Shore had stayed in London with her friend and former colleague Nurse Mabel Rogers. On receipt of a late-night telegram Rogers rushed down to Hastings and remained at her friend's bedside until she succumbed to her injuries, at 7.55pm on Friday 16th January.

The famous pathologist Sir Bernard Spilsbury came to Hastings on 18th January to examine the compartment and conduct a post mortem. It revealed that the injuries had been 'inflicted with enormous force and caused catastrophic damage'. At the inquest Coroner William Glenister remarked that it was 'exceedingly hard that a lady of this character whose life had been devoted to others should lose her life under these distressing circumstances'. The foreman of the jury was blunter: he called the attack 'a cowardly and dastardly act'.

Early in the morning of 20th January, Miss Shore's coffin was taken to Christ Church in London Road, where a sombre requiem mass was held. A large number of local people came to pay their respects, including clergy, town councillors, nurses and Red Cross workers. A motor hearse took the coffin to London. By this time the public knew about the murder of a war heroine, and The Times reported that, as the cortège passed, 'Large crowds lined the streets and a large force of foot and mounted police was needed to control them'.

Hastings Police, Scotland Yard and the railway police began a joint investigation. Nurse Rogers recounted how, on 12th January, she had accompanied her friend to Victoria and settled her into an empty third-class single compartment with no corridor, just an exit door at each side. Miss Shore

Florence Nightingale Shore.

Nurse Shore (left) with her friend Nurse Rogers.

Atmospheric photo taken in 1914. The East Sussex Hospital is on the left. The cupola on the right marks the entrance to the pier.

had about £3 in her purse and was wearing a gold wristwatch, one ring of gold and another of platinum with diamonds and a sapphire, and a gold necklace with an amethyst pendant. These were absent when she was found, suggesting robbery was the motive, although her luggage and handbag were present and had not been ransacked.

Nurse Rogers told the police that, just before the train left, a slightly-built, clean-shaven man in his late twenties had entered the compartment. She noticed that he wore no overcoat, despite the cold weather. Guard Duck explained that at Lewes his train was two coaches longer than the platform. He saw a man open a door near the back (the Hastings portion) and edge along the running board until he reached the platform, then walk away. He resembled the man Nurse Rogers saw, except he wore an overcoat. Despite that discrepancy he was the prime suspect, so it is a great shame that he was never traced.

After three inquest hearings, on 2nd March the verdict of the Hastings jurymen was 'murder by some person or persons unknown'. A few suspects were questioned, one was arrested and released, and two who confessed turned out to be fantasists.

Miss Shore left £14,279, worth over a half-a-million pounds today. Her habitual self-denial and frugality that led her to buy the cheapest ticket may have cost her her life.

The Nightingale Shore case is filled with tragic irony. Working in war zones whilst bombs fell all around, she placed herself in mortal danger from enemy attack for years, and emerged unscathed only to be murdered in peacetime in her own country in a railway carriage en route to the seaside.

The case remains unsolved and is the subject of a full-length book by Rosemary Cook (*The Nightingale Shore Murder*).

References: *HSLO* 24th January 1920; *The Times* 21st January 1920.

Hollington Church-in-the-Wood.

1927

Corpse-in-the-Wood

Hollington

On Sunday 18th December two brothers set out to gather moss in the ancient woods near their home. William Lee, twenty-one and Joe, a month short of eighteen, were out of work and Joe had appeared in Hastings Magistrates' Court six times for theft and burglary, for which he had twice been birched. They lived in a cottage at 22 Hollington Old Lane with their father (a pig dealer) and mother (a door-to-door hawker).

As they reached a remote part of the 100-acre wood, about half a mile north-west of Church-in-the-Wood, the underwood was, in Joe's words, 'A lot taller than I am, and very thick. You have to bend to make a way through'. He spotted something unusual which, on closer inspection, turned out to be a rotting left shoe containing human foot bones. He noticed several larger bones and some shreds of fabric. Luckily, the brothers had the sense to leave their gruesome discovery intact. Joe hastened to the police station and brought Inspector Robins and PC Manktelow to the chilling scene.

The remains were hundreds of yards from the nearest cart track and even further from any footpath, which explained why they lay so long undisturbed, as few summer ramblers would venture so deep. After conducting a thorough examination of the remains and searching the surrounding area, the police officers collected everything connected with the deceased into a bag and took it to nearby Cowslip Farm, the residence of Count Paul Ignatieff.

Dr John Kendall of Battle inspected the remains. It was clear that the corpse had been exposed for a long time, he thought (incorrectly) upwards of two years. Because the bones were devoid of flesh, it was impossible to ascertain the cause of death. Asphyxiation, drowning and poisoning, for example, leave no evidence on bones. They showed no signs of violent attack and no discernible fractures, but many were missing: one collar-bone, six ribs, the left shoulder bone, seven vertebrae, the left tibia and fibula, both hands, and the right foot. The extremities (right foot, hands, upper spine, and tail bone) had been gnawed by animals, probably foxes or weasels, which were surely also responsible for carrying away the skull, which was found a few yards away.

Looking for clues to the identity of the deceased, Kendall examined the few fragments of clothing present. There was some white material (maybe a vest), rotten and stuck to the bones; a piece of dark blue fabric with a white pinstripe (possibly a skirt), attached to the left thigh bone, whilst on the right thigh bone was a small piece of underwear. One leg bone had a remnant of thick,

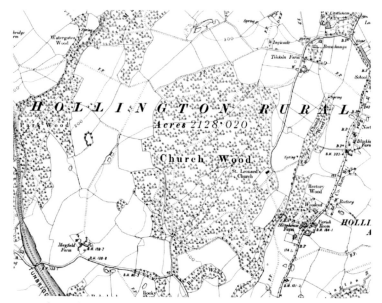

The ancient woods north-west of St Leonard's church, better known as the church-in-the-wood. The area has since been developed and the spot where the remains were found falls somewhere between Sidney Little Road and Ingleside.

dark stocking attached. The left foot bones were inside a shoe with a fairly high heel. Printed onto the inner lining were the words 'Super Easiephit', a large footwear manufacturer with nation-wide retail outlets. The teeth provided the only glimmer of hope: the lower jawbone was intact and contained a vulcanite plate with six artificial and six natural teeth. An upper plate of eight false teeth was found close by. The artificial teeth were gold-mounted, indicating a certain level of wealth, so she was unlikely to have been a tramp, down and out or a lower domestic servant.

Kendall told the police that the deceased was a female of between thirty and forty. No woman in Hastings was registered as a missing person. The police composed a description of the false teeth and the scraps of clothing, and circulated it to forces across Britain.

The Coroner for the Rape of Hastings, Frederick Sheppard, had taken over the job from his father, Charles, who held the post for fifty-four years. From the age of seven he would attend his father's inquests, then, as a young man, he studied for the Bar. Returning to Battle he was deputy coroner from 1914 until his father's retirement in 1919, when he stepped neatly into his shoes.

Count Paul Ignatieff allowed the inquest to be held at Cowslip Farm. On Wednesday 21st December Mr Sheppard heard depositions from Joe Lee, PC Manktelow and Dr Kendall, then adjourned for a fortnight. He submitted the false teeth to a jaw pathologist for special examination, hoping it might lead to identification. When the inquest resumed (at his office in Battle) on 7th January,

Sheppard was gratified to hear that a Southampton policeman, upon reading about the discovery, remembered a forty-year-old widow had gone missing a year earlier. He requested the dentures, and these led him to a local dentist called Duncombe.

Mr W.G. Duncombe attended the inquest. The upper denture of the false teeth bore his crescent-shaped mark, and he recognised the lower plate. He had made them on 19th March 1924 for a Mrs Emma Frances Cozens, of Spring Road, Southampton. He had never met her; he was given the job by another dentist.

Emma Cozens, née Cooper, was a shy, unassuming woman who lived with her parents till she was thirty. In 1916 she married a workmate of her brother, a joiner in the shipyard. The death of her husband had left her heartbroken and she was still in mourning in 1926, three years later. Although she had her own home, where she carried on her trade as a dressmaker, she disliked spending evenings alone there and dreaded sleeping in an empty house. Her mother and brother Norman lived together a few minutes' walk away, so she spent her evenings there and stayed over, and every morning she walked home, with her beloved dog, to perform her dressmaking work.

Emma seldom went out socially, and a trip outside Southampton was a much-talked-about event. She told her two older sisters, brother and mother all her plans. For example in early November 1926 she said she was going to Portsmouth to attend a Sunday afternoon lecture by the travelling preacher, Rev Geoffrey Studdert Kennedy. Known as 'Woodbine Willie', he was a Christian socialist and champion of the working classes. Emma heard his talk, 'Reaction and Revolt', a critique of capitalism and greed, then returned to her mother's house and spent the evening and night there as usual.

The next morning, Monday 8th November, over a lengthy breakfast, Norman said he wanted to go out a couple of evenings that week; he asked Emma if she would be able to look after their mother, who was elderly and infirm. She made no mention of any plans to go anywhere. At 8.45am she and her dog set off as usual. About two-and-a-half hours later, the dog returned alone.

Norman walked him to Emma's but she was out. Using his key he took a look around. Everything seemed normal. She had definitely been home: her long black skirt and dark grey raincoat were gone. When Emma did not turn up by the evening, Norman reported the circumstances to the police. Hearing of her mysterious disappearance a lady came forward to say she had seen her on a tram on the morning of 8th. She alighted at the Cattle Market, but Emma had remained on board. Southampton station was the next stop.

After thirteen months of anguish, not knowing if she were dead or alive, the Coopers were told that Emma's remains had been found. At the inquest, Norman accepted that Mr Duncombe made the teeth, but not for Emma, despite his records bearing her name and address. Producing a photo, Norman pointed out her unusually large jawbone. Mr Duncombe said it matched the one found in the woods. Norman argued that the striped fabric did not match any item of Emma's: 'She never bought a thing she did not show my sisters', he said, 'and they can't remember her ever possessing a blue skirt, or anything blue, especially with a stripe in it'. The coroner suggested it was the lining of her raincoat.

Mr Sheppard accepted Mr Duncombe's record as evidence of identity and the jury returned a verdict of 'found dead'. Details of Emma's funeral were not published, nor can I find any trace of her grave. She left no will but her brother applied for probate. Her estate amounted to £313 (about £17,000 today).

❊ ❊ ❊

The only answer to the mystery offered by the *HSLO* was that Emma 'lost her way in the woods, and, becoming faint from fright and exhaustion, collapsed and lay there till she died'. The *Hampshire Telegraph* ended its brief report by implying suicide: 'The dead woman had been depressed by the death of her husband'. Both solutions were presented as though there was no need to explain how, or why, she was in Hollington Woods.

Let us imagine that Emma had decided to travel ninety miles to take a stroll alone in the dark, in woods she had never visited before. First, without reason, she concealed her day-trip from her family. She left Norman at 8.45am, walked home, grabbed her raincoat and took a tram to Southampton station. The next train to London was the 10.22 to Waterloo, arriving at 12.22, and the next to St Leonards was the 1.20pm from Victoria. Arriving at 3.40 she had to locate the tram stop and travel three miles to the woods, arriving between 4.15 and 4.30. To get home the same day she would have to be back at the station in time for the 7.12 to London. Then she would take the 10pm to Southampton, arriving home at 1am.[1] This absurd scenario would entail fifteen hours of travel in order to spend two hours wandering alone in a strange wood, with only a thin raincoat to protect her from the cold, stumbling about in the dark through half a mile of trees, stumps, moss and thick underbrush — in a pair of high heeled shoes.

Emma was too timid even to sleep in her own home alone; the thought of walking alone in the dark through strange woods would have terrified her. If she intended to be out for fifteen hours she would have told her brother not to expect her for dinner and asked him to tend to her dog.

With regard to the suicide theory, whilst it is true that she was in mourning, Emma was getting on with life, working, and going out more. Her close-knit family, who saw her daily, had no fear that she might harm herself. If she planned suicide, of all the methods and locations at her disposal, this was the least likely. The planning and concealment showed not impulsiveness but forethought, and yet she left no will, no note, and no provision for her dog. Lastly, if she longed to die in the woods, the New Forest was on her doorstep.

---

1. According to the 1922 timetable, which will not have changed much by 1926.

Ruling out accident and suicide leads inevitably to the conclusion that another person killed Emma. She may have arranged to meet up with a new man friend, but kept it from her family because it was new and she was shy about it and wanted to avoid the barrage of questions that close-knit families always ask. Something may have happened on that date that ended with her being killed and hidden so deep in Hollington Woods that nobody found her remains for a year. If she was on a date, why was her dog wandering the streets alone?

As in the chapter 'Indian Clubbing', the dog in this story is something of a 'smoking gun'. Whether Emma was going on a date, enacting her planned suicide, or staying out till 1am, she would have made arrangements for her dog. She could, for example, have left him with her brother after breakfast on 8th November, saying she would collect him later.

There is only one theory that can explain every point and tie up every loose end: Emma was abducted and taken to Hollington by road. Perhaps she went home, put on a warmer skirt and a raincoat to take her dog for a run in the park, and was snatched from there. Her dog, eventually realising he had been abandoned, toddled off to one of the homes he lived between. Statistically this explanation is unlikely, partly because at that time only 2% of the population owned a motor vehicle, plus another 2% could borrow one or used one at work (e.g. van, lorry or taxi drivers, chauffeurs). Abductions, kidnappings and stranger-murders were extremely rare, but nevertheless, they did happen.

For example, in 1921 Thomas Allaway sent a telegram to Irene Wilkins, a stranger to him, who had advertised looking for work. He lured her to Bournemouth with the offer of a job, and collected her at the station using his employer's car and wearing his chauffeur's uniform. He then drove her three miles, beat her to death with a hammer and dumped her body in a field. This scenario sounds utterly implausible — more like the unrealistic plot of a novel. And yet it really did happen and Allaway, who admitted to the murder after being found guilty, was hanged in 1922. The case proves that it is not beyond the realms of possibility that Emma was abducted or lured to her death by a stranger, maybe even a 'copycat' killer familiar with the Allaway abduction.

References: *HSLO* 24th Dec 1927; 7th January 1928; *West Sussex Gazette* 5th January 1928; *Hampshire Telegraph* 6th January 1928; *Montreal Gazette* 3rd January 2009.

Digression: Paul Ignatieff

Count Pavel Ignatiev, anglicised as Paul Ignatieff, was born in 1870, the son of the Minister of the Interior under Tsar Alexander III. He studied at the University of Kiev and married Princess Natalia Meshcherskaya in 1903. Under Nicholas II he served as the Governor of Kiev, then headed the imperial ministries of agriculture and, later, of education. During the 1917 October Revolution he faced execution, but his life was spared because a Polish commissar remembered that, whilst education minister, Ignatieff had secured for Polish people the right to retain their own language.

The count, countess and their five sons fled Russia on a British warship in July 1919. They set up a dairy farm in Paris, then moved to Hollington, where they bought a nine-bedroom manor house called Beauchamps (which they renamed 'Kroupodyorka') with a tennis court, an orchard and a cottage. They also purchased an adjacent 200-acre dairy farm, then known as Tilekiln, which they changed to Cowslip Farm (to avoid confusion with another dairy farm in Ore with the same name). They opened a tea garden with 'glorious views', providing breakfasts, luncheons and suppers for the many excursionists and hikers who visited Hollington Woods.

The Ignatieffs did not expect special treatment or attempt to capitalise on their aristocratic ancestry. They lived and worked just like any other dairy farmers, caring for their herd, selling their products and occasionally entering a hen in a poultry competition. In addition the count shared the benefit of his special knowledge and formal training by giving educational public talks about farming and agriculture.

One of the Ignatieff sons moved to Canada and his letters home prompted the rest of the family to want to join him. Beauchamps, including its entire contents, and Cowslip Farm were offered for sale in early 1929. Cowslip Farm later reverted to its former name and Beauchamps became a hotel and then 'Buckets & Spades', a Jewish holiday home for mentally handicapped children.

By 1930 the Ignatieffs had moved permanently to Canada. During the Second World War their son Vladimir became a lieutenant in the Calgary Highlanders and was, by sheer chance, posted to Sussex. One day in 1941 his unit was sent to Hollington, where he had spent seven years of his youth, and he found himself eating a 'haversack lunch' near the Church-in-the-Wood, surrounded by land once owned by his parents.

Beauchamps when it was a holiday home.
A map showing Beauchamps and Tilekiln Farm (Cowslip Farm).

1928

Dying for a Pee

Filsham

In 1904 Welsh-born Charles Tasker, principal of a private school in London, married Alberta Stromeyer, proprietor of a millinery shop at 52 King's Road, St Leonards. Although in their mid-forties, it was the first marriage for both and they were very happy. They lived in London until 1918, when Mr Tasker reached the age of sixty, then retired to Hastings.

But retirement did not suit Mr Tasker. His active mind and passion to impart knowledge continued unabated. He embarked on a new venture: he leased a house called Craig Ard, which was situated between 15 and 17 Elphinstone Road. Here he set up a private school to tutor boys by the hour or the term, and also to accommodate a few boarders. Sadly, his wife died in 1922, but he carried on teaching and boarding pupils, assisted by a housekeeper.

In 1927 Mr Tasker downsized to a spacious flat within Castledown House, a former rectory and took only hourly pupils. Although pushing seventy, he was strong, physically active and enjoyed excellent health. On 18th July 1928 he took a brisk walk to Hastings station and purchased a third-class return ticket to London. He returned on the 10.05pm express, entering the rearmost single compartment of the first carriage. The only exits were a door on each side, fitted with sliding latches that could be operated from inside or out.

At Battle, Porter Albert Sargent walked the length of the train to ensure that every door was shut and securely fastened before the train left. At West St Leonards Porter Edward Morris entered a compartment. He noticed that both doors and both windows were firmly closed, and someone had left behind a hat, a newspaper and two magazines. There was nothing to suggest that, barely two minutes earlier, a man had either jumped or fallen out onto the track.

At 9.25 the next morning Sub-Ganger Percy Austin was walking the line south-east from Crowhurst when, one-and-a-half miles short of West St Leonards, he found a man lying on a slope 14ft from the rails. He was unconscious and bleeding. A St John motor ambulance conveyed him to the Buchanan Cottage Hospital, London Road, where he drifted in and out of consciousness, unable to explain what had happened. He had fractured his skull and pelvis and sustained multiple other injuries, from which he died on 23rd July.

Marks at the scene revealed that he had fallen onto the ballast in one place then walked or crawled thirty yards along the track — losing his fob-watch and chain, his keys and a pretty silver matchbox on the way — before tumbling down an embankment.

Nobody exited the compartment at West St Leonards, and the door latches were tested and had no defect. So, he was not pushed and he did not fall. He must have opened the door between stops. But why? The combined brainpower and forensic expertise of police, doctors and railway inspectors could not solve the mystery.

Only one person advanced a theory, and that was the coroner, W.J. Glenister.[1] He suggested that Mr Tasker 'opened the door *for a purpose*'. The single compartment in which he travelled had no access to a WC and the journey had taken nearly two hours. He was two weeks short of his seventieth birthday, maybe his bladder could not hold out even two more minutes until the next station was reached.

Mr Glenister concluded that 'the circumstances of the poor man's death were not known and never could be known'. He expressed 'sorrow and regret' that 'a man who bore a most admirable character should have come to his death in this way'. The result of the inquest was 'very unsatisfactory', and he directed his jury to find an open verdict.

Mr Tasker was buried with his late wife in the Borough Cemetery on 26th July. He left all he had (£93) to his housekeeper.

References: *HSLO* 21st July, 28th July & 29th September 1928.

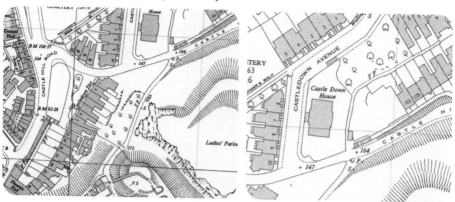

Castledown House, said to be haunted by the famous tragedienne actress Sarah Siddons (right), who had no connection with Hastings, but who died in 1831, the year it was built for William Wallinger. He was the curate of the private chapel of St Mary-in-the-Castle, whose associated cemetery is opposite. After lying derelict for many years the house was demolished in the 1970s. Modern dwellings cover the site, and perhaps residents have seen the ghostly image of Mrs Siddons.

1. William Joseph Glenister (1850–1929), the son of W.M. Glenister, the first chief constable of Hastings, was the senior partner of Davenport Jones & Glenister, solicitors. Charles Davenport Jones had been coroner before him, and Jones's son Harry took over from Mr Glenister.

1929

FREAK WAVE IN A HEATWAVE

THE HARBOUR ARM

Saturday 20th July was a day of sultry and oppressive heat. The slight breeze barely disturbed the sea but caused a few ripples on the shore. Children paddled at the water's edge, small boats floated languidly and day-trippers sauntered along the prom, bathed, or sat in deckchairs reading newspapers or licking rapidly-melting ice-creams in the brilliant sunshine.

William and Lilian Pollard, a married couple in their mid-thirties, and their friend Percy Williams, all from Woking, were determined to have a fun weekend. They checked in with their landlady at Lavender House, 2 Rock-a-Nore Road and enjoyed a light luncheon. Making their way to the Hastings Sea Angling Club, they booked a fishing trip. At 3pm Boatman Edwin White and Percy Williams took an oar each and rowed out to sea. All three were enthusiastic anglers and they fished for over three hours. Only when they ran out of bait did they reluctantly head back to dry land. An eloquent reporter from the *HSLO* described what happened next:

> Dense black clouds gathered from the west and piled themselves up into leaden and silver ridges. A gentle breeze that scarcely ruffled the surface of the sea changed without warning to a howling gale, and holiday makers made a wild rush from the beach and parade to shelter. People on the Front were caught unawares when the wind sprang up. In a minute hats were blown off, parasols were turned inside out, and newspapers were torn from readers' hands. Placards and display boards outside the White Rock Pavilion were blown down the steps. It was only this grim omen of what was to come that prevented an appalling death toll.
>
> The wind died away with the uncanny suddenness with which it sprang up and the air seemed electric with a sense of foreboding.
>
> Then the phenomenon happened. An immense bank of water, estimated to be 20 feet high, mounted from the calm sea and rushed towards the shore with incredible speed. It was dead low tide at the time and the wave tore up the almost deserted beach for a distance of nearly 50 yards. What would have happened if the beach had been crowded can be left to the imagination. The wave receded as rapidly as it had advanced, leaving a handful of onlookers gasping with astonishment.

About 20 minutes after the tidal wave appeared the rain pelted down with tropical fury and everything was blotted out as though by a mist. The downpour, which was accompanied by vivid lightning over the sea and dull rumblings of thunder, lasted for a quarter of an hour.

Mr Wilkins, a pier official, said: 'I saw what looked like a white wall of water, about fifty feet high, stretched along for about three-quarters of a mile. I don't think anyone here has ever seen its like before.' Near to his viewpoint on the pier, a speedboat hit the wave at forty miles an hour and tipped almost perpendicular, leaping twelve feet into the air.

Opposite Warrior Square the wave caught a skiff and carried it over the rocks, turning it keel upwards and lurching all three occupants into the water. They were rescued by bathing attendants, who waded in up to their armpits. Two paddling children were engulfed and lifted by the wave then flung several yards along the beach, where, still submerged, they were rescued by an attendant. After the first wave a local boy, Jack Reynolds, was left marooned on a rock. A few seconds later he was again buried in a mass of roaring foam. PC Marchant ran into the sea in full uniform, and as he reached the spot the water receded to reveal little Jack clinging to the rock like a limpet.

Boatman White had worked on the sea nearly all his life and had seen every type of weather. He had twice narrowly escaped being drowned when vessels capsized, and in 1904 had been rewarded for bravery after helping to rescue the crew of a wrecked fishing boat. He explained:

> Nothing like it has ever happened at Hastings before. The wave came upon us like the wall of a house, and over we went. We all went under once, and it seemed minutes before I came up. The rebound from the shore was worse than the actual wave.

The *HSLO* said: As 'the tidal wave rose with phenomenal suddenness out of a placid sea', the little fishing boat was 'caught in a seething mass of foam and tossed about like a cork, while the four occupants, bewildered by the blinding

TIDAL WAVE TRAGEDY.

—:o:—

BOATS ENGULFED IN HUGE WALL OF WATER.

WOMAN VISITOR DROWNED.

THRILLING RESCUE SCENES AT HASTINGS.

HOLIDAY MAKERS DASH FOR SAFETY.

spray, struggled for their lives in the water.' William Pollard described what happened as the boat reached the break in the harbour arm:

> The sea was like a millpond, but it was beginning to darken and we expected a storm. The boatman said 'Here comes the wind,' and there was a gust shortly after. Then the wind came with a full blast from the south-west. We were within ten yards of the shore. If it had been half a minute later we should have reached the shore. All of a sudden the boatman said: 'My God! What's this coming?' I looked round and saw a high wave approaching. We have been in some rough seas, but we have never seen a wave like that before. There was no chance of avoiding it. The boatman turned the boat's stern square-on to the wave so that it did not catch us broadside-on.

Percy Williams added,

> There was no warning. I was facing the wave when it approached like a wall. I should think it was about 30 feet high. It broke right on us and we were thrown into the water. The backwash was worse than the actual wave, as there was more tide in it. The first time when we came up we were all close together, then another wave came and threw the boat over again and we became separated.

After the second wave, Percy clung onto the capsized boat whilst White kept afloat by holding an oar. William Pollard found his wife face downwards in the water, turned her over and kept her head raised until help arrived.

The fishing party was rescued by Boatman White's brothers Jack and George, Vic Price and others. Mrs White, who happened to be on the beach, endured a nail-biting wait as they rowed out to the stricken anglers. Vic dived into the sea and passed Lilian up to his mates in the boat, then the three men were hauled aboard. The group was rowed ashore, where police had formed a cordon to hold back a crowd of gawpers. After first aid was rendered by Dr A.T. Field, ambulancemen and fishermen, the men quickly recovered but, despite prolonged artificial respiration and the administration of oxygen, all efforts to revive Lilian failed.

At the inquest a verdict of 'death by misadventure' was returned. Coroner W.J. Glenister asked Boatman White: 'You have seen a good many squalls at sea, but you have never seen anything like that?' White replied: 'Never in my life, sir, nor heard of one', and agreed that he 'would never have believed it possible'.

In his summing-up the coroner declared: 'I have never heard or read anything of this character in my life. No one can explain the cause of it, but it will no doubt be the subject of anxious investigation by meteorologists and scientists'.

Reference: *HSLO* 27th July 1929.

Poster for the Hastings stop of the 1930 tour, showing Kumasi, a Bengal tiger that Adolph's father Karl had trained to ride a horse.

Karl with the tiger, three lions and two polar bears on a poster for the Olympia show.

Artist's impressions of Adolph and the polar bears at Hastings. *Illustrated Police News.*

1930

BORN TO BE WILD

CAMBRIDGE ROAD

Bertram Mills spent the 1920s 'raising the status of the circus to heights hitherto undreamed of'. He sought artistes of the very highest calibre until he had assembled the finest acts for his famous circus, which ran at London's Olympia exhibition centre for ten seasons, being enjoyed by thousands, including film stars and royalty.

Mills engaged several members of the Cossmeyer[1] family, Czechs who were famed across Europe as circus animal trainers. Adolph was born in Prussia on 23rd February 1902 and, as a child, 'exerted an uncanny influence over wild beasts'. When he left school he took a degree in Medicine and Law at the University of Prague and learned to play the violin. However, after graduating he was irresistibly drawn back to the 'family business', to which he dedicated the rest of his life.

By his late twenties Adolph was 'a trainer of world renown' whose animals were 'completely subjugated to his will' by 'the soothing, almost hypnotic power of the soft intonation of the voice'. The three essential foundations of his success were the study of animal psychology, sympathy and utmost patience. He never forced or bullied an animal and, unlike others, performed without a whip, a prong or a concealed knife. John S. Clarke MP,[2] a former lion tamer, asserted that Adolph was 'possibly the greatest wild beast trainer of his age', and Bertram Mills lauded him as 'one of the cleverest trainers in the world'.

Mr Mills recruited Adolph in December 1929 and his 'big cat' act quickly became the most popular feature in his circus. 'Slight in build, ascetic in appearance, with alert eyes and quick movement', Adolph performed inside a giant cage with 'nine huge lions who do his bidding with but little persuasion'. He also trained his father Karl's four polar bears, and after they performed a set of tricks for the audience, pretended to give one a kiss (in fact the bear was taking a sugar cube from his lips). Karl had been known as 'Cossmy' for years, but soon people began using the nickname for Adolph.

After a decade in London, in 1930 Bertram Mills decided to take his hugely successful circus around Britain, determined that the touring show would be equal in quality to the fixed one, he hand-picked the cream of his performers, including Karl Cossmeyer and his sons Adolph and Alphonse.

1. The family sometimes spelled the name Cossmayer or Kossmeyer.
2. John Smith Clarke (1885–1957) was Labour MP for Glasgow Maryhill from 1929 to 1931.

THE DESPERATE STRUGGLE

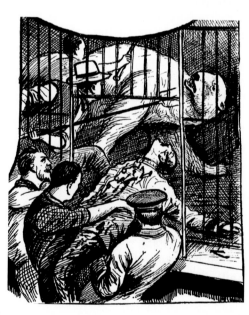

'THE ANIMAL JUMPED ON HIS SHOULDER'

Artist's impressions of Adolph being attacked by the polar bear, from the *Illustrated Police News*.

On Sunday 17th August 'Bertram W. Mills' Circus and Menagerie' arrived at The Oval on Cambridge Road and erected a huge tent (the 'Big Top'). The spectacular three-hour show ran daily at 3pm and 8pm, from Monday 18th until Saturday 30th. It featured 'a galaxy of artists from across the globe', a 'glittering array of thrilling acts', including 'aerial butterfly sensationalists', a human cannonball, a pair of boxing midgets and the 'unrideable mules', which were guaranteed to provoke a 'mirthquake'. After each performance the public was invited to view the menagerie, 'an unequalled collection' of lions, tigers, brown and polar bears, and 'other species gathered from jungle and plain'.

On the morning of 29th August, Adolph and the bear-keeper, Richard, entered a cage to give a polar bear its daily shower. After dousing it with a hose, they began to shampoo its fur with soap. For no apparent reason the bear suddenly rose on his hind legs and bit Adolph in the neck as it pushed him to the floor. The bear's huge bulk crushed him and pinned him down as it savaged his face, chest and arms with its claws and teeth. Richard tried to pull Adolph out of the cage but the bear had hold of its trainer's leg. Richard jabbed at it with a two-foot prong; soon, others join in, prodding it with wooden poles poked through the bars. Eventually it retreated into a corner, 'growling with rage'. Karl joined Richard in rescuing Adolph from the cage and, after laying him gently onto the grass, saw the full extent of his dear son's horrifying injuries.

An urgent call to the RESH brought Dr Francis Daunt, Dr Irene Rogers and Sister Jones to the scene in a motor-car.[1] Adolph had sustained ghastly injuries unlike anything they had seen before. The poor man had thirty separate wounds. His face, neck and throat bore gruesome lacerations; one eye had been clawed out, his nose and one of his ears had been bitten off, and his spine was broken. By some miracle, he was alive. Kneeling on the grass the team dressed the injuries as best they could, closing the most widely gaping wounds with loose stitches. An ambulance rushed him the two hundred yards to the hospital, where 'everything possible was done'. Within half an hour Adolph Cossmeyer, one of the world's finest wild animal trainers, lay dead in a Hastings hospital. He was just twenty-eight.

As a mark of respect to the man he called 'one of the cleverest trainers in the world', Bertram Mills cancelled both performances that day.

Because the circus was leaving on Sunday, the post mortem was carried out immediately and the inquest was squeezed in between the two Saturday performances. A member of the troupe acted as interpreter for those witnesses who knew no English, and their appearance in court wearing circus costume provided a unique experience for Coroner Charles Davenport Jones. Karl was devastated by his son's death. Adolph had trained, performed with and helped look after the bear for five years, and it had never been aggressive.

A verdict of 'death by misadventure' was returned.

1. Francis Eldon Daunt (1889–1952) and Irene Heloise Rogers (1898–1993).

After the inquest came the explanations for the bear's aberrant attack. Mr Davenport Jones, who had received anonymous letters about wild animals in captivity, opined that polar bears were 'very uncertain in temper'. Dr Geoffrey Vevers, superintendent of London Zoo, called them 'notoriously untrustworthy creatures'. Circus performers were sure it was simply a case of 'brute force used in rough play'. John S. Clarke had a theory, which he expressed eloquently:

> [Adolph] slipped on a piece of soap, and in falling his elbow caught the bear a severe blow on the snout. Here was the first pain ever inflicted by a gentle master, but the wild beast cannot reason. All the cunning and ferocity hived in that shallow skull from generations of grim, stark struggle in the frozen north sprang suddenly to activity.

On Sunday 31st August the Big Top was dismantled and the touring circus was packed away and taken by road to Hove. The bear continued to perform, which outraged the Captive Animals' Defence League. They wrote to the Home Secretary about the public wanting to see the bear that killed a man. They wanted it returned to its natural habitat, or destroyed, but the state had no power to take either action.

The fate of Adolph Cossmeyer's body is a mystery: his death was registered in the normal way, and he should have been buried either in Hastings or in Brighton & Hove, but I can find no record of a funeral or a grave anywhere.

References: *HSLO* 9th & 23rd August and 6th September 1930. *Daily Herald* 24th November 1930. *Illustrated Police News* 4th September 1930. John S. Clarke in the *Daily Record* 4th September 1930. In his 1937 book *Circus Parade*, Clarke claims he saw the attack; in fact he was not in Hastings on that day.

Adolph giving a bear a sugar-cube kiss.

1932

Indian Clubbing

Eversfield Place

At 6.44am on Wednesday, 20th July a young man approached the front desk at Hastings Central Police Station and told Sergeant Nice: 'Someone has murdered my wife. I went back to get my dinner and found her dead.' He was very distressed and crying, so Nice got out the smelling salts. When he regained his composure, the man gave his name as Arthur Harman, and the address of a basement flat on Eversfield Place. PC Diwell and PC Sheppard were despatched immediately.

Upon reaching the seafront building at 6.55am, the pair peered over the stone balustrade and viewed the basement area. Nothing seemed amiss so they unlatched the iron gate, descended the curved stone steps and opened the unlocked front door. A black retriever approached them, barking loudly, but allowed them to enter unmolested. On the floor in the hallway lay a bloodied Indian club. Through the open door of the front room they saw a baby in a cot, awake but quiet, and a teenage girl in bed, apparently asleep. She lay on her side and only half her face was visible because the sheets and blankets were pulled up level with her ears. When Constable Arthur Diwell drew back the bedclothes he saw her head covered in blood. She was dead, but her body felt warm.

The police surgeon, Dr A.T. Field, arrived soon afterwards. He established that she was lying down in a sleeping position when attacked and had not been moved since. Apart from the head injury, the body showed no marks of violence. He put the time of death as between 6am and 6.30.

At 7.25am Detective Inspector George Knell[1] and Detective Sergeant Cox drove to the scene in a police motor-car (the HSLO dubbed them the 'Flying Squad'). They examined the flat. It was neat and tidy throughout, and comprised a bedroom, a box room, a kitchen and a scullery which led to a small, fully-enclosed back yard. The back door was closed but not locked, and the small yard was surrounded by high walls and a cliff. Without a ladder and access to a neighbour's yard, the only way into the flat was via the front door or the adjacent sash window, neither of which showed any sign of forced entry. There was no evidence of an intruder and no sign of a struggle. The girl's handbag contained 6s 6d and there was £3 17s (about a week's wages) in a cash box in the wardrobe. The murder weapon was probably the Indian club, as it bore blobs of blood that were still sticky. The clubs always came in pairs and, sure enough, its twin was found inside a cupboard.

1. DI Knell was head of CID from 1928 until 1944, when he was promoted to superintendent.

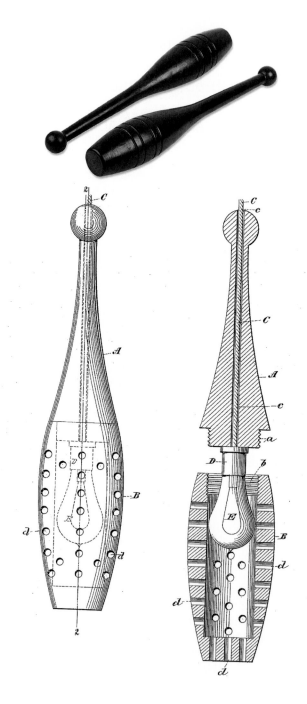

Indian clubs, and how they are constructed.

Indian clubs had at that time been in use for about a century. Weighted inside, they were the forerunner of today's barbells and were used primarily for strengthening the arms. 'There's nothing better for the arms than Indian clubs, unless it is a blonde', quipped *The Tatler*. Some used them at home; others in gymnasia, and P.E. groups gave displays of synchronised Indian club-swinging.

After the scene was photographed by Mr A.M. Breach, the baby was taken to hospital by the St John Ambulance Brigade, the retriever — 'howling restlessly' — was walked to the police station, the club was despatched to Scotland Yard for fingerprint tests and the body was removed to the mortuary.

Back at the station the distressed young man, Arthur Harman, had been waiting anxiously in the parade room. When Sgt Nice confirmed that his wife was dead he broke down and sobbed. After giving up his clothes for forensic examination he enquired after his baby girl, who was fourteen months old, and provided addresses for his and his late wife's parents.

Just over two years earlier Mabel and Charlie Hicks had two teenage daughters, Beryl and Queenie. Now, both were dead. When Beryl was just sixteen — and four months pregnant — she married Bernard Hobden, aged twenty-four. Beryl died in May 1930 from a complication of childbirth, and Mabel was raising the baby. Queenie was two years younger than Beryl and her tragically short life echoed that of her sister. Three months after Beryl's funeral Queenie, just fifteen, became pregnant by Arthur Harman, a lorry driver six years her senior. Harman had committed statutory rape, but the police did not prosecute if the couple subsequently married. The wedding took place at Hastings Register Office in March 1931, two months after Queenie's sixteenth birthday, and the baby was born two months later. The following summer Queenie was dead and another baby was deprived of its mother.

When police visited Mabel's home in Guestling and broke the dreadful news, she was 'overcome with grief'. She and Charlie were legally separated so police went to his lodgings at 123a All Saints' Street. Though deeply upset he agreed to formally identify the body at Rock-a-Nore mortuary.

Arthur Harman, born in Guestling in 1909, was the seventh of eleven children.[1] His family lived for some years at Sailor's Stream, a thatched cottage at Three Oaks, and he started his working life as a labourer at Shearer's dairy at Doleham Farm, Brede. In 1928 became a motor-lorry driver for Carter's, a haulage contractor based at Sedlescombe Road North in Baldslow, and by 1932 three of his eight brothers were also employed there.

After their marriage Arthur and Queenie shared a tiny terraced cottage in St Leonards with Arthur's sister, her husband and their two babies. 2 Eastern Street[2] contained only 'two up, two down' and a scullery. After Queenie's daughter

1. Arthur's grandfather John was the father-in-law of Ann Harman, the victim in 'Chair Trigger'.
2. The alley to the left of the Oak Bakery on London Road used to be the entrance to Eastern Street, which then ran east and ended where the car repair shop is today.

Eversfield Place in the 1930s.

Location of the police station after 1881. The entrance was opposite Middle Street.

was born in May 1931 the overcrowding was intolerable and so, in September, the Harmans moved into a flat of their own. Above it were an optician's surgery and more flats. Queenie, though only sixteen, was appointed caretaker of the building, which brought her a small wage. Just as the couple had reached a good situation with both home and work, Queenie was murdered.

DI Knell.

According to Harman's formal written statement, as taken down by DI Knell, he rose at 5.20, made hot cocoa and carried a cup to his wife, ate his breakfast and prepared his packed lunch (which he called 'dinner'). Returning to the bedroom he gave the baby some warm milk and kissed Queenie goodbye as she lay in bed. He left the flat at 5.50 or 5.55, crossed the road and boarded a Maidstone & District trolleybus (the conductor later verified that it left Harman's stop at 6.07). Alighting at the Victoria Hotel[1] on Battle Road at 6.23, he walked along a footpath to Park's Hill and thence to Carter's garages at Baldslow. He managed his usual ten-minute walk in just seven minutes, arrived at Carter's at 6.30 and left in his lorry at 6.32. Realising he had left his dinner behind, he drove home to collect it.

Harman's account contained discrepancies. He left home before 5.55, and the stop was opposite his home, yet he failed to catch the 5.58 bus. He found Queenie with the bedclothes over her head, but there was no blood on that part of the sheet. When police searched the flat they found no packed lunch. Harman claimed that the club in the hallway was usually stored in the shed under the front steps, a damp, dusty place full of mould and cobwebs, yet apart from the blood it was perfectly clean.

The timings of his movements between 6.32 and 6.44 were impossibly tight. He left Carter's at 6.32 and the drive home took seven or eight minutes, placing his arrival at 6.39 or 6.40. He claimed that, in no more than five minutes, he carried out the following actions: parked the lorry, crossed the pavement, descended the steps, unlocked the front door, entered the hallway, paused at the bedroom door to explain his surprise return to Queenie, waited for a response, approached her, pulled back the bedcovers and established that she was dead, walked through the hall and out of the front door, closing it behind him, climbed the steps and crossed the pavement, got back into the lorry, started it up and drove three-quarters of a mile to Robertson Street, where he passed a policeman at 6.42, then drove around the Albert Memorial and into Middle Street, parked the lorry, climbed out, walked some yards to the police station and up to the front desk, presenting himself to Sgt Nice at exactly 6.44.

1. Built on the site of the Victoria Inn featured in 'The Cook of Caterina Villa' and now a Co-Op.

Hastings Police in 1928. In the parade ground behind the town hall.

1930s police cars at the entrance to the station on the west side of the town hall.

DEATH TRAGEDY IN
A BASEMENT.

HUSBAND REMANDED.

Innocence Plea in Wife
Murder Charge.

Arthur Edward Harman (24), a
lorry-driver, of Eversfield Place, Hastings, was charged at Hastings, to-day,
with the murder of his 17-year-old wife,
Queenie Winifred Harman.

Poor images of Arthur and Queenie Harman from the *HSLO* and *Daily Herald,* and a clipping from the *Yorkshire Evening Post,* 21st July 1932. The story made headlines across Britain.

DI Knell visited the chief constable's office at intervals during the day, drip-feeding his boss the results of the initial investigation and his interview with Harman. Mr James authorised him to charge the young man with the murder of his wife. When he did so, just after 6pm, Harman replied, 'I swear on God's honour I did not do it'.

Word swiftly got around town and on Thursday 21st July scores of locals and holidaymakers queued outside the town hall, determined to get sight of the monster who murdered what the press called his 'Girl-Wife'. Among them were Queenie's brother and sister, aged thirteen and eleven. When the doors opened the crowd surged forward and the court filled up rapidly, but the public gallery was closed and many were turned away. The most determined loitered outside, prepared to wait as long as necessary to catch a glimpse of Harman as he left.

After the magistrates dealt with some lesser offences, at 11am he was ushered into the dock. A strikingly handsome man, Arthur Harman looked smart in his double-breasted, grey flannel suit, even though his shirt lacked a collar and his fair hair was tousled. On the solicitors' table lay a long wooden case containing the Indian club. Chief Constable James read out the charge: 'Arthur Edward Harman feloniously, wilfully, and with malice aforethought, did kill and murder' Queenie. As DI Knell described finding the body Harman sank in his seat and buried his head in his hands. The police asked for a week's remand to complete enquiries. When the clerk asked if there was any reason not to remand him, Harman rose to his feet and 'seemed tongue-tied for a few moments'. He 'swallowed hard as he tried to frame a reply'. Then, 'visibly affected by the ordeal through which he was passing', he confirmed that everything in his statement was true, adding, 'I know I am innocent'.

The crowd waiting patiently outside was left unsatisfied because Harman did not emerge. Instead he was taken down the internal stairs to a police cell and given his dinner. Later he was handcuffed to a policeman and taken by train to Lewes, where he was held in prison until the hearing.

Medical and forensic reports showed that Queenie died of 'asphyxia due to blood passing into the lungs consequent of a fracture of the skull'. The Indian club could have caused the injury. Dr Lawrence Philip Blayney Chamberlain, a pathologist at the RESH, found six traces of blood on the club and twenty-six on Harman's handkerchief (which Harman attributed to a nosebleed). Coroner Harry Davenport Jones[1] held a brief initial inquest hearing, issued a warrant for burial and adjourned the proceedings until 2nd September.

On Tuesday 26th July Queenie was buried next to her sister in the churchyard of St Laurence at Guestling where, nearly a century earlier, three other murder victims had been interred.[2] The mourners were outnumbered by a large contingent of inquisitive strangers. None of the Harman family attended, but a wreath of ox-eyed daisies bore the inscription: 'In loving memory, from Arthur to Queenie, my dear wife, Mrs Harman.' After a short address by the new rector, Rev Hubert Evers,[3] the simple coffin was interred next to Beryl's grave.

Two days later, Harman made his second court appearance. Again large numbers were unable to gain admittance because the public gallery was closed. Harman's solicitor, John Cyril Bosley, an eager young man from Brighton, was only six years older than his client. He applied for and was granted legal aid for Harman, who was remanded for a second week. The next hearing was held over two days: 4th and 5th August, Harman spending the intervening night in a cell beneath the police station. Magistrates had to decide if there was enough evidence to send the case to trial at the Lewes Sessions.[4] On both days a queue of several hundred formed outside the town hall. Although the public gallery was opened it soon filled up and most were turned away.

When Harman arrived he was 'in good spirits', chuckling at a remark passed between police officers and smiling to his relatives at the back of the court. When the murder charge was read out he immediately became serious and 'stood stiffly to attention'.

Mr H.J. Parham, appearing for the Director of Public Prosecutions, thought it extraordinary that Harman drove nearly a mile to a police station when a GP lived three doors away. Swift medical attention may have saved his wife's life. He read out the statement made by Harman on the day; from the

---

1. A son of Coroner Charles Davenport Jones; both of them appear in other chapters.
2. See 'The Family Poisoner'.
3. In the 1940s his wife Dr Effie Evers upturned a white marble slab that lay in her pantry and discovered, to her surprise, that it was a commemorative tablet inscribed to Dr Elizabeth Blackwell. The riddle of how and why it was there is, as yet, unsolved. Known as the Guestling Tablet, it was donated to the Royal Free Hospital, where it was placed into an archway.
4. The first day's bench comprised Dr Locke, William Perrins, J.N. Collins, Walter Jezzard, Edmund Harden, John Boutwood, Edward Heron, Major Cyril Davenport and Mrs Hannah Edwards; on the second day Collins and Jezzard were replaced by George Holt Ormerod and Frank Slack.

outset he had tried to insinuate that another was to blame. 'My wife has got one or two enemies', he had claimed, 'but I don't know their names'. He continued:

> She has been keeping company with two or three young men, two of them are married. About a fortnight ago I was near Hastings Pier with my wife when she pointed one of the young men out to me who she said she had been keeping company with, but I don't think I should recognise him again. I told my wife at the time that I did not mind her walking out with him if she kept true to me ... About a fortnight ago I got her some stout and she had a drink of it at night, and the following afternoon she went to get the remainder. When she drank it straight from the bottle it burnt her throat. She said something had been put in the bottle but she had destroyed it before I got home. She had made herself sick and was all right afterwards ...
>
> When I first got married we had one or two rifts, and she threatened to run away from me, but we have been getting on all right this last nine months. I let her go out two evenings a week on her own, and when she goes out I look after the baby.

The prosecutor pointed out that no complaint had been made to the police about any 'attempted poisoning'.

Mr Parham suggested that Harman could have murdered Queenie at 6am, taken the 6.07 bus to work and then driven straight to the police station without going to the flat. To support this theory, several witnesses who had passed the Harmans' flat at around 6.40 gave evidence. None had seen a lorry parked outside. One was a trolleybus driver who could fix the time he passed at precisely 6.39. When asked by defence solicitor Mr Bosley whether he was 'sufficiently confident ... to let it be accepted as evidence against a man charged with murder', the driver replied firmly: 'I am, sir'.

Milkman Henry Santer passed the flat between 6.35 and 6.40 and saw no lorry, either parked, arriving or leaving. Mr Bosley asserted that, doing the same round every morning, he could have mixed up the days. Ada Skinner, a maid at the Alexandra Hotel, saw Santer's milk cart but no lorry when she stepped off a bus at 6.40. When Mr Bosley suggested that she, too, had her days muddled, she broke down in tears and was ushered out.

Sergeant White saw Harman's lorry travelling east along Robertson Street at 6.42. This did not prove he started from Eversfield Place; had he come from Carter's he could have taken a route that also ended in Robertson Street. Regarding the absence of blood on Harman's clothes, if he had driven straight from Carter's to the police station he had enough time to get changed en route and throw away any stained clothes.

Pursuing the line that Queenie was murdered in a jealous rage, Mr Parham set about proving that Harman was frantically possessive and his wife an incorrigible flirt. Two of Queenie's cousins gave evidence. Eighteen-year-old Caroline Foster, daughter of Queenie's maternal aunt, Hettie Furminger, took

The hoarding to the right of the Spider's Web restaurant reads 'John Carter, Haulier' and marks the slip road into his garages, from where Harman collected his lorry. Jewson's now covers the site.

the stand. Queenie had once said, in front of Arthur, that she had been to a cinema with Gordon Overington. Arthur had warned her: 'Be careful what you are saying, Queenie'. About six weeks before that, Arthur told Caroline he 'had been having a lot of trouble about Queenie'. Caroline told the court that she 'knew something would happen'.

Winifred Morgan, another maternal cousin, was seventeen and lived at Council Cottages, Broad Oak. She described a dispute 'two or three months earlier', when the ill-fated couple lived in Eastern Street. Queenie wanted to cross the road to speak to a young man with whom she was acquainted, and Harman had physically prevented her from leaving the house. Mr Bosley discredited Winifred's testimony because the Harmans had moved out of the cottage in Eastern Street nearly a year previously.

Ronald Knight used to work in a china shop on the corner of Eastern Street and London Road. One day Queenie had chatted with him and later on Harman had stormed in and threatened him: 'If I ever catch you again talking to my wife there will be trouble.' Gordon Overington, a carpenter, was an acquaintance of the Harmans. Whilst he was working on a house in Kenilworth Road, Queenie visited him on three consecutive days. On the fourth day Harman called on him and said: 'My wife and you are getting too friendly. Will you leave her alone, and me as well, and not see us again?' Overington denied taking Queenie on a date to the cinema. They had simply watched the same film at the same screening. She had paid for her own ticket and they sat separately.

Concluding for the defence, Mr Bosley called the evidence 'a shadowy mass of weakness, on which the prosecution suggests that this man should be condemned to death'. He continued: 'There is very little to connect him with this offence ... Not a single fingerprint has been produced and there is not a single bloodstain that accuses him'.

After the magistrates retired to discuss the case 'an excited buzz of conversation ran through the court'. Minutes later, as they filed in to resume their places on the Bench, the public fell silent and 'a pin could be heard to drop'. The presiding magistrate announced that the evidence was insufficient to put Harman on trial: 'The prisoner is, therefore, discharged'.

According to the *HSLO*, 'Thunderous cheers echoed' through the court. Harman smiled broadly and 'a terrific roar of cheering broke out from the gallery and the well of the court. Men and women jumped to their feet waving their arms excitedly.' Harman was overwhelmed by the outpouring of jubilation, and 'once he reached the quietude of the parade room he gave way to the terrible strain'. Several hundred people 'packed the pavement and roadway outside the police station waiting for Harman to appear', explained the *HSLO*. 'When he stepped through the door they cheered themselves hoarse ... women kissed him and men shook him by the hand'. Harman, 'flushed and smiling', walked off with his relatives 'the sound of cheering still ringing in his ears'.

A week later the *HSLO* reported:

> Hastings police are leaving no stone unturned to bring to justice the murderer of Queenie Harman ... detectives have re-opened investigations and are exploring every possible avenue that is likely to shed fresh light on the mystery. Since the murder they have taken over eighty statements from various people.

The police did not produce any other suspect and the investigation was closed. A few days later the *HSLO* stated that, under the Coroners (Amendment) Act of 1926, the adjourned inquest would not be resumed. No explanation was given.

Why did the magistrates decide not to send Harman for trial? Apart from one woman, the bench was made up of elderly patriarchs aged between sixty-five and seventy-seven; men born in the 1850s and 60s, when wives were completely subjugated to their lords and masters. Did their deep indoctrination lead them to subconsciously believe that wives who flirted 'deserved' the consequences, or could they not bring themselves to send a hardworking young man to a trial that could end with his death on the gallows for obeying his primordial instincts, his nature-driven, and therefore uncontrollable, reaction to his wife's constant infidelities?

If Harman did not kill Queenie, then who did? Someone she knew? A random stranger?

At 1.50am on 2nd July, eighteen days before Queenie was murdered, Nellie Hailstone was asleep in a front basement room a few doors from the Harmans when an intruder attempted to break in. She shouted and he ran away. Her sister went to her own flat (next door to the Harmans) to call the police and a man was arrested and charged with loitering with intent to commit a felony. He could have returned to the area, found the club in the shed under the steps, lifted and climbed through Queenie's bedroom window, and bludgeoned her as she snoozed. An unprovoked, motiveless, random, murderous attack on a stranger was so rare that, statistically, she had more chance of being struck by lightning. What is more, had an intruder entered without rousing Queenie, her dog would have barked and woken her. Dogs are famously protective of their owners, and the Harmans' retriever was a particularly vocal one: it barked loudly at the police when they arrived and throughout the morning as strangers came and went. Therefore it follows that the assailant can only have been someone who could approach Queenie with the dog's blessing.

In addition to the inaction of her dog, the fact that Queenie was either asleep or lying down relaxing in bed limits who the murderer could be. If someone known to Queenie had paid an early-morning visit, she would, at the very least, have sat up in bed to converse with them.

Statistically, the vast majority of murders are committed by someone known to the victim, and most female victims are killed by their male partners. All too often, when such cases come to court, it emerges that the man acted out of feelings of entitlement and ownership. In many cases his partner was about to leave him. Queenie flirted with other men, prompting Harman to become possessive and resentful. Maybe they had a furious row about it that morning; perhaps Queenie told him she was leaving him, provoking the typical response of possessive husbands, past and future: 'If I cannot have her, nobody can'.

The theory that Harman killed Queenie ties up every loose end and resolves every contradiction. It explains why the dog failed to bark a warning when he approached his mistress, and the timings work perfectly: Harman assaulted her at about 6am, caught the 6.07 bus, collected his lorry at 6.32 and drove to the police station. He did not go to the flat, which is why he did not fetch the nearby GP and why no witness saw his lorry outside.

Most telling of all, it explains why Harman failed to do what any father would after finding his wife brutally murdered: protect his child. Every parent's instinct would be to remove the baby from the flat; instead, he left her alone, with the murder weapon a few feet away. He did not even check the flat to see if the intruder was still on the premises, nor lock the front door.

Only one person knew for certain that the assailant would not return and kill the baby: the murderer. Partly for this reason, but also because of that other 'smoking gun' — the dog — I believe that Harman murdered his wife.

Epilogue: The fate of Arthur Harman

After his release Harman spent a week with his parents at 2 Great Maxfield, Guestling. He refused to return to work because he could not bear people asking about Queenie. Moreover, he was ostracised, and people were gossiping about him and staring at him in the street; some even whispered hurtful things as they passed. His employer, John Carter, had recently accepted a contract to supply haulage lorries to East Sussex County Council, which was building the A2270 northwards from Eastbourne. Carter assigned Harman to the job so he could escape Hastings. Arrangements were made for him to lodge with 'Ned' Kelly, an elderly labourer, at County Council Bungalows (ex-army huts) at Polegate. Harman showed Ned a photo of Queenie and press cuttings about the case, which he always carried with him, saying that 'everybody thought him a murderer'.

In May 1933 Harman began romancing Doris Avery, who lived at Milton Street, a hamlet three miles away. She assumed he was single but one day, after she teased him about other girls, he fell silent and broody. Later he told her about Queenie and, from that day forward, asked 'on many occasions' if she thought him a murderer. 'Sometimes he would plead with me to trust in him and believe in his innocence', she said.

After a brief courtship Harman proposed and their wedding was planned for December but, becoming increasingly scared by his possessiveness, Doris called it off. She would have stopped seeing him but he threatened to 'do himself in' because she was 'all he had to live for'. When he warned her that he had a gun she gave in to his emotional blackmail and agreed to remain friends.

When Harman visited Doris's family home on 11th February 1934, her male cousin was staying, which made Harman jealous, and he also objected to her attending a dance. Her reminder that they were no longer engaged provoked another row and she said it was better to stop meeting. Harman assured her it would be the last time she saw him. The next morning, instead of going to work, he visited again and stayed three hours. Despite parting with the words: 'You will not see me again', he returned at 8pm and stood on her doorstep in silence. After a while he asked for a glass of water, which Doris gave him, reminding him again that it was over between them. At 8.15 he asked her to kiss him, saying it would be the last time he would 'worry her'. She obliged, and he left.

Harman failed to return to County Council Bungalows that night. On Tuesday 13th February at 8.30am his body was discovered by Albert Sayers, a railway platelayer inspecting the line from Berwick to Polegate. It was on the up line, about a yard from Folkington Bridge, face down, both arms tucked underneath the torso. Most of the body lay on the outside of the line but the head was in the four-foot way (the space between the rails). Harman must have placed his neck on a rail and waited to be decapitated by the wheels of the next train. Sayers called the police and helped them to remove the deceased to the Horse and Groom Hotel at Polegate, where Harman's grieving father was brought for the gruesome task of identifying his son's mutilated remains.

The inquest was held at the hotel on 15th February by Dr Edward Fitzwilliams Hoare, coroner for East Sussex. When Doris gave her deposition Dr Hoare sympathised, assuring her that she was 'perfectly within her rights' to break things off with him. His wife being murdered had probably made him 'different mentally from other people' and even a relatively small upset, such as he had with Doris, might have been 'sufficient to unbalance his mind'. The jury returned a verdict of 'suicide while of unsound mind' and expressed sympathy with his parents. Two days later Arthur Harman was buried in the churchyard of

St Laurence in Guestling, in the same grave as Queenie. No member of Queenie's family attended or sent flowers.

One of the Harman brothers had recently married and it seemed natural for the newlyweds to take in Arthur's orphaned baby. Having the same surname, neighbours doubtless assumed she was their daughter. They later had a son and raised the pair as siblings. It is possible that the girl was never told she was adopted, for it would have been too painful for her to hear that her mother was brutally killed and her father, having been accused of her murder, had committed suicide in such a ghastly fashion.

References: *The Tatler* 24th August 1838. *Yorkshire Evening Post*, 21st July 1932. *HSLO* 2nd, 23rd & 30th July, 6th, 13th & 27th August 1932 and 17th February 1934; *Eastbourne Gazette* 14th February 1934; (clipping below) *Evening News* 6th April 1934.

TRAGEDY OF YOUNG
Widower ·

HAUNTED BY MEMORIES
OF MURDER.

"Terrible Jealousy."

A 25-YEAR-OLD widower, haunted by the fear that people thought he had murdered his girl-wife, was found dead on the railway line at Polegate in Sussex.

Less than two years ago this young man, Arthur Edward Harman, was accused at Hastings of the murder of his 17-year-old wife. She was found dead in their St. Leonard's home with her head terribly battered. Nearby was a blood-stained Indian club. Harman protested his innocence at the police court proceedings, and the magistrates found there was not sufficient evidence to send him for trial. He was discharged.

Harman, an extremely handsome young man, had many friends. His married life was happy until his jealousy threatened to wreck it. When the tragedy came along he brooded. Then romance came to him again. He fell in love with Doris Avery, of Polegate, where he was working as a lorry driver. Miss Avery told their story at her mother's cottage.

1932

DON'T TRY THIS AT HOME

SEDLESCOMBE ROAD SOUTH

Arthur Sladden was born in Ashford in 1916 to Ada Rosa Victoria Jessie Sladden, an unmarried teenager. Raising a child alone in the 1920s was a daily struggle, and it is to Ada's credit that Arthur grew up to be a healthy, happy, adventurous boy with an ambition to join the Royal Navy and train as a shipwright.

By 1932 Arthur was fifteen and at 5ft 9in towered over his mother. They lived at Brittany Cottage on Sedlescombe Road South with her boyfriend, a chauffeur called Sidney Reginald Vere. Arthur had a passion for action and adventure films and would go anywhere to see his favourite swashbuckling actor, Douglas Fairbanks: the Silverhill Picture House, the Elite on London Road, the Kinema on Norman Road, the Cinema de Luxe at Pelham Place or the Plaza All Talkie Theatre in Cambridge Road.

> Douglas Fairbanks's stunts included jumping to incredible heights in *Robin Hood* and *The Thief of Bagdad*, thanks to hidden trampolines on set, skimming down a sail in *The Black Pirate* on the point of his dagger, and completing parkour-style rooftop chases in *The Mark of Zorro*.

Arthur would return from the cinema and emulate his hero. He told his mother he longed to 'climb up walls', but she disapproved of his experiments with ropes, pulleys and a long leather belt: 'I told him he would break his neck', she explained, 'but he only laughed'. Sidney described the boy as 'very impulsive'; he, too, had warned against trying to copy dangerous antics seen at the picture houses, but he would wait until Sid was out and do them anyway.

On Sunday 15th May, when Sidney and Arthur were in the kitchen making breakfast, the boy was in particularly high spirits. Later Sidney was in the garden when his attention was drawn to their outside toilet: a leather strap had been poked through two ventilation holes at the top of the door and tied in a knot. He knocked and called Arthur's name but there was no reply, so he forced the door open. The boy was on the inner side of the door, naked from the waist up and hanging by his neck, which was in a noose formed by a long leather belt threaded through the holes. He was half kneeling, with only his toes touching the floor. Sidney quickly sliced through the belt with a sharp knife and carried the unconscious boy into his workshop. He could not feel a heartbeat and, as neither he nor Ada had any idea of how to perform artificial respiration, she put a call through to the nearby Buchanan Cottage Hospital.

Dr Ethel Lee arrived within minutes but Arthur was already 'very blue'. She started artificial respiration, and was soon joined by Dr D.J. Martin, Dr G. Nesbitt Wood and Dr Frederick John Cutler, who brought oxygen. The four did everything in their power to revive Arthur, but it was too late.

P.C. Capelin examined the scene. One end of a long leather belt had been passed through the buckle, forming a noose. The end had been poked through the ventilation holes in the toilet door and tied in a knot to stop it slipping out. The holes were about 5ft 6 from the ground and a large chopping block on the floor was probably what he had used to stand on.

The post mortem, made by RESH pathologist Dr Percy Lazarus-Barlow, showed that death was due to 'asphyxia and cerebral anemia resulting from a constriction round the neck'.

An inquest was held without a jury by Coroner Harry Davenport Jones at Silverhill Council Schools. After hearing from the witnesses, he remarked that the case was an extraordinary one. Clearly, Arthur had become so obsessed by the methods of his idol Douglas Fairbanks that he removed his vest and shirt and tried to climb up the tall toilet door. Why he had placed his neck in a noose was more of a mystery. 'I must say frankly', he concluded, 'that this puzzles me and I propose to find an open verdict'.

References: *HSLO* 21st May 1932. Quote - *The Guardian* 7th September 2015.

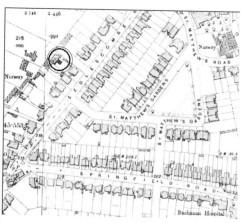

Brittany Cottage (circled) and the Buchanan Cottage Hospital.

Douglas Fairbanks in *The Thief of Bagdad*.

Mystery Walk

River Brede

Frank Eldridge had a happy life, despite its inauspicious beginnings. His mother, one of eleven children, grew up in rural poverty in Westfield, where, as an unmarried teenager, she gave birth to Frank in 1863. She died when he was a baby, and he was raised in Murgy Pit Lane, Icklesham, by his Uncle William, a master bricklayer who apprenticed him. Frank decided bricklaying was not for him and moved to Hastings, where he secured a job as a carman, delivering groceries to customers in a horse-drawn van.

In 1890 he married Alice Hall and began married life in rooms at 139 Queen's Road before settling long term at 8 Earl Street, a neat, bay-windowed, five-roomed terraced house. Frank was a well-liked, amiable man, a church-goer and a steady, reliable employee. Family life was peaceful, conventional and uneventful. All eight children survived to adulthood and the twin boys even managed to serve in the Great War without getting killed or injured. The couple were gratified to see their offspring leading useful lives and making good marriages; one girl wed an engine driver, another married the landlord of the Queen Adelaide in Rye; one of the twins joined the police force, the other became a railwayman.

When Frank was sixty-five he was knocked down by a motorcycle and was treated for concussion. From that day, 'when he stooped his hand felt funny, and when he laid down at night there was one side he could not lie on for long'. Apart from that minor niggle, as Frank entered his dotage he was in exceptionally good health and his fitness was well above the average. His income increased when he turned seventy because he was entitled to draw an Old Age Pension and also worked as a house-painter for John Lester and Co, a building contractor of high repute.[1] He had no worries and still loved his wife after forty-five years of marriage.

On Saturday 23rd February 1935 Frank went missing.

Charles Eldridge, a shop assistant in his forties, had joined his parents that day for dinner. His father was his usual, cheerful self and, being a creature of habit, at 8pm he left the house for his nightly 'constitutional' walk. He always returned by 10pm, but this time he did not and nobody had a clue where he was.

---

1. Lester's was based in Earl Street and employed over 100 men. It built the *Observer* offices, schools and a chapel, and was contracted to repair many Hastings landmarks.

On 16th March a shepherd discovered a dead body lying face downwards in less than two feet of water in the River Brede, on Court Lodge Farm, Udimore, about a mile from Icklesham. With assistance he dragged the body out. It was an old man, fully clothed complete with a hat, but no overcoat. The Udimore police constable and a doctor from Rye attended. There were no signs of violence and the man had not been robbed; in his pockets were a silver watch and a purse containing 15s. The police soon matched missing person Frank Eldridge to the unknown corpse, and Frank's son Charles identified the body.

The coroner for the Rape of Hastings, Mr F.C. Sheppard, held an inquest without a jury. The post mortem had shown the cause of death was suffocation by drowning, and the condition of the body was consistent with having been immersed in river water for three weeks, so Frank probably died the night he went missing.

Nobody could comprehend why, on a cold winter's night, Frank had walked for twelve miles, through town and country, across empty, icy fields and soggy marshland, then wandered around in pitch black darkness until he fell into the River Brede. If he had slipped or tripped, why did he not simply extricate himself? The water was not even two feet deep. Presumably he must have been unconscious. Charles said that, whilst his father was familiar with the area during his childhood, he had no living relatives or friends there, and had not visited the district for decades.

Mr Sheppard concluded that there was 'no evidence that this is a case of self-destruction', but equally 'no evidence which satisfies me that it was an accident'. He returned an open verdict.

Frank Eldridge was interred in Hastings Borough Cemetery. His family lived the rest of their days never comprehending why he went to Udimore, nor how he came to drown in the shallow waters of the River Brede.

References: *The Times* 18th March 1935; *HSLO* 23rd March 1935.

1935

Riddle of the Range

White Rock

During the First World War, Spencer Bransby's mother brought him and his little sister Beryl to live in Hastings whilst their father served in France. After the war they decided to stay and added two more children to the family.

Spencer, who was born in November 1910, was a musically gifted child who at age six had gained the highest marks in England in a piano competition. He and Beryl, who was four years his junior, possessed fine voices, sang duets at parties, and took part in concerts for children. Spencer and his father, Archie, joined the Hastings Players Amateur Operatic and Dramatic Society. From his debut, aged ten, in J.M. Barrie's play 'Quality Street' at the Gaiety Theatre, Spencer appeared for fourteen years as a supporting actor or chorus singer. Archie played leading parts in many productions and in 1927 produced two plays at St Leonards Pier, casting his daughters as dancers. Both girls performed in various amateur productions, Beryl in particular being in demand as a dancer, solo vocalist and choreographer.

Whilst taking part in the Battle Abbey Pageant in July 1932 Spencer met Patricia Murtagh, a fellow cast member. Romance blossomed quickly and they married just eight weeks later at Holy Trinity church. The newlyweds moved in with his parents and maternal grandmother, who had plenty of space for them in their twelve-roomed home, Wykeham House, 98 Braybrooke Road. In February 1933 the couple, along with Beryl, sang in the chorus of 'Iolanthe' at the Cinema de Luxe; Archie was the Lord Chancellor and his nine-year-old son Gordon played his page. On 16th July Patricia had a son, Norman.

Spencer was fascinated by motor cars, which in his lifetime had rendered horse-drawn vehicles obsolete. After studying the internal combustion engine, in 1932 he landed a job as an engineer and salesman at a company in Eastbourne. Three years later he was taken on by D.M.S. Motors at 2 Mercatoria, closer to home. In the spring of 1935 Spencer bought a car. Summer was coming and he wanted to be able to take his darling wife and dear little son, who was approaching his second birthday, on trips to the countryside.

At school, Spencer had been an all-round sportsman, excelling at cricket, football and swimming; as an adult he took up shooting. He and Archie joined the Hastings Volunteer Rifle Club, the Sussex County Rifle Association, and the shooting club at the Palace Chambers Rifle Range. Although only twenty-four, by 1935 Spencer was already on the committee at the Palace and among the club's best marksmen, having won the Stubbs Cup for the previous two years.

Sketch of the Gaiety Theatre printed on a 1926 programme. Spencer Bransby made his debut at the theatre at the age of ten. It is now a cinema.

Members competed for the cup every May and so, on Tuesday 9th April, after the usual shoot, five stayed behind for extra practice. Spencer volunteered to 'spot' for the other four, announcing where each shot had hit the target. His eyesight was so sharp he could 'spot' without binoculars.

The range was in a cave cut into the sandstone cliff; the targets were lit but otherwise the range was in complete darkness. The four marksmen — Eric Good, Frank Coates, Bert Standen and Leslie Cornelius — lined up behind a wooden school form. They were shooting with miniature rifles from a standing position at targets about 20 yards away. Spencer stood to their left and crouched down as the marksmen's eyes were focussed on the gunsights and targets. They each began to fire shots, then suddenly Spencer reeled backwards and collapsed on the ground. At first his mates did not know why he had fallen, and approaching him were horrified to discover that he had been shot in the back of the head. One dashed out for medical help but, minutes later, Spencer died in the arms of the club secretary, Leslie Cornelius.

The police undertook a thorough inspection and questioned everyone present. DI Knell took away all four rifles, each one clearly labelled with the name of the man who had been using it; he also took the ammunition and the targets. Spencer's body was removed to the mortuary, where Dr G. Nesbitt Wood conducted the post mortem and sent the bullet, along with the labelled rifles, to Dr Davidson, director of the Metropolitan Police Laboratory at Hendon.

White Rock in the 1930s, the Palace Hotel is the tallest building, in the centre, and the rifle range was at the rear, on the ground floor.

PC Dann was detailed to carry out the saddest duty. He had to visit Wykeham House and inform a young wife that her husband was dead and her toddler fatherless, as well as having to break the news to the man's parents. The following day Archie faced the dreadful task of formally identifying the body of his beloved son.

The inquest opened at the town hall on 12th April. After evidence of identification was taken, Coroner Harry Davenport Jones issued a burial order and adjourned for three weeks to allow the police to complete their investigation. The next day Spencer's name appeared in the HSLO on the league table of the Sussex County Rifle Association. He had gained top marks.

Each of the marksmen endured nearly three weeks of anguish, waiting to hear which of them had fired the fatal bullet. During that time they attended Spencer's funeral on 15th April. The service at Christ Church, Blacklands, and the interment at the Borough Cemetery were well attended by family, friends, neighbours, colleagues, members of rifle clubs and concert parties, sports associations and representatives of the Hastings Players. As the cortège passed Ore church the bell was tolled as a mark of respect.

Meanwhile Hastings Police had investigated a theory that a rebounding bullet may have been responsible. Although the cave was sandstone, there were steel fittings from which a bullet might ricochet. However, nothing was found.

The town was shocked by the death of someone so young, and felt deeply for his widow and baby son. Sadly, some nasty people spread baseless rumours around town, claiming that Spencer had shot himself. At the resumed inquest on 1st May, Mr F.G. Beckett, solicitor for the rifle club, issued an emphatic public statement to refute the lies. The coroner also quashed speculation by stating that there was 'not the slightest tinge of possibility' that it was suicide. The truth was that Spencer had inadvertently raised his head, placing it momentarily in the line of fire. It was an accident, and no blame could be placed on anybody.

Forensic evidence proved that the bullet had been fired by Frank Henry Relph Coates. Coates had every reason to bury his head in his hands and say 'Oh no, not again'. Ten years earlier, when he was just eighteen, he was driving his employer's two-seater Ford motor-car at 10mph along Havelock Road when Percy Tubbs, who was crossing the road without looking, walked straight into his path and — despite the low speed — was killed. No blame was attached to Coates, who, despite the shock the two fatal accidents must have caused him, lived to the age of ninety-one.

Archie continued to shoot at the Palace Chambers. In his son's memory he presented the club with the Bransby Cup in 1936. Archie moved the family to London. His children's final performance was 'Scenes from Shakespeare' at the Concordia Hall in 1939. Spencer's widow remarried and left Hastings but, years later, her son Norman returned with his own son to his birth town. He was very fond of cricket and, in a reprise of his grandfather's gesture, presented the Jeanette Bransby Trophy for services to the sport, named for his wife.

References: *HSLO* 24th September 1932, 13th April 1935, 4th July 1936.

Digression: the Nesbitt Woods

Gordon Nesbitt Wood (1904–1984), who appears in several chapters, was one of a pair of doctors with the same surname. In the early 1920s he met fellow medical student Cordelia ('Delia') Helen England (1905–1989) at Cambridge University. They both qualified MA, MB, MRCS and LRCP then worked in London hospitals for a few years (he at Guy's; she at King's College).

They married in 1930 (the year these photos were taken) and became partners in a GP surgery at 45 Wellington Square. By 1934 Gordon had been appointed police surgeon for Hastings and Delia deputised in his absence. During the Second World War Gordon's absence was of several years' duration, as he served as an army medic on field ambulances in France. Delia replaced him as police surgeon throughout the war and also carried out all the necessary post mortems. She continued as his deputy after his return.

Throughout their long and useful careers each Dr Nesbitt Wood held various honorary positions; Gordon served on committees whilst Delia taught first aid classes. They had no children but shared exciting hobbies: both gained pilots' licences and he was a skilled sailor. When they retired in the 1960s, each had served Hastings for thirty-five years.

1939

THE PIERMASTER'S SECRET

HASTINGS PIER

Eric Mumford was born in Hastings in April 1904, the middle of three children. His grandparents ran a seafront lodging house at Denmark Place; his father was a linotype operator for the *Hastings & St Leonards Observer* at its printing works in Claremont. Eric grew up at 3 Wellington Terrace, Portland Place, until 1922, when he and his widowed mother moved to 193 Queen's Road. Ten years later she left Hastings and he rented rooms at 18 Cornwallis Gardens.

From his teens to his death, Eric was employed on the piers, where he acquired the nickname 'Jack'. He was perfectly suited to the work because his character was a blend of sociability and reliability. Starting as an attendant at the bowling alley on St Leonards Pier, he rose, over a decade, to be deputy master of Hastings Pier, 'ever ready with suggestions for improvements, and the ability to help in carrying them out'.

Hastings Pier had been managed by a master since it opened in 1872. The role carried heavy responsibility, particularly during the 1930s, when its workforce of almost a hundred supervised, served and entertained three-quarters of a million people every year. In 1932, during Jack's tenure as deputy, the pier celebrated its diamond jubilee, and over the August Bank Holiday weekend its staff had to cope with 60,000 visitors.[1]

The pier was particularly well patronised by those seeking musical and theatrical entertainment. Since 1931 it had boasted an excellent resident dance orchestra — Alan Green and his 'boys' — which had previously topped the bill at the London Palladium, enjoyed a residency at the Royal Opera House, and made eighteen recordings. In the early days Alan used to say that Piermaster Teddy Down and his deputy Jack deserved to join the band on stage and take a bow, for it was their idea to 'give the public what they wanted, instead of trying to educate them with highbrow music'. Although Alan was a decade older than Jack they became best pals.

The pier was Jack's life. Apart from attending functions at his Masonic lodge, he even spent much of his leisure time there, enjoying musical performances by night and fishing off its seaward end by day. During sea-angling festivals he was appointed the pier's honorary chief fishing steward.

Clad in a smart, naval-style, double-breasted suit and a white-topped nautical peaked cap encircled with gold braid, Jack cut a dash with his handsome

1. Visitor numbers were known because in those days entry was by twopenny admission ticket.

Mr. " Jack " Mumford.

*Of duties grave and gay or queer,
I might have sung a sonnet.
But all of you know Hastings Pier,
Well. he's the master on it.*
J. R. C.

This is the first of a series of well-
known local personalities, caricatured by
Donald B. Cameron, who is now associated with Messrs. Berre and Brown, the
Hastings scenic artists.

Photos and a drawing of Jack from the *HSLO*.

face, manly, upright figure and neatly trimmed, brilliantined hair. A charming and well-liked man, he was rarely seen without a broad, toothy grin and a witty comment on his lips. He was on excellent terms with his employers, his colleagues and the public, and was even invited to be best man at the wedding of a local policeman bobby. He even liked his boss, calling him his 'loveable chief'.

But the job was not all about appearances and popularity. Jack was also competent and resourceful, and displayed courage and a deep sense of duty to protect the public, no matter how reckless. He could not swim, and yet, one day in 1934, after a drunk jumped off the pier, colleagues had to intervene to stop him from launching a rowing boat into the rough sea to rescue him.

When Teddy Down retired in April 1938, after forty-five years with the pier company and thirteen as piermaster, Jack stepped smoothly into the top job. A few weeks later he was deeply saddened to hear that Mr Down, for whom he had 'the deepest feelings of regard', had died.

That summer visitor numbers broke all records, and at weekends the pier was so crowded with people that Jack struggled to get from one end to the other.

By then Jack was the most instantly recognisable person in town. On 6th August he became the first 'local celebrity' spotlighted in a new 'People You Know' feature in the *HSLO*. To accompany a sketch of him someone had composed a silly rhyme: 'Of duties grave and gay or queer, I might have sung a sonnet, But all of you know Hastings Pier, Well, he's the master on it.'

A war with Germany had been anticipated for years. A local air raid committee had been formed in 1935, and from January 1938 the RAF conducted training exercises involving mock bombing raids. By October 47,000 gas masks had been distributed and air raid sirens installed all over town. Further precautions and plans were put in place throughout 1939 and from August the seafront illuminations were switched off at night.

For those in the world of showbiz it was 'business as usual'. The late summer programme for the White Rock Pavilion included the Fol-de-Rols (featuring Cyril Fletcher and his 'Odd Odes'), 'the famous BBC comedian' Leonard Henry, and Billy Cotton's Band, lauded as 'Europe's greatest'. On the pier the Revellers concert party was delighting audiences in the theatre every evening and in the pavilion on two afternoons a week with their show 'Laughter Unlimited'. Alan Green's hardworking dance band performed at 11am daily and at 3pm on five days, and also provided the music for dances every night. Sunday evenings at 8pm the band joined forces with the Revellers for a 'grand double feature' in the theatre.

In July 1939 Jack Mumford and Alan Green were interviewed by the *HSLO*. They were feeling 'jubilant' because they were organising a grand 'Hastings Night' to be held at the Royal Opera House in London that autumn. The Borough Association was financing the scheme, a Hastings song was being composed, and a charter train would take locals to London to see the show. Brimming with excitement, the pals expected over 4,000 people to attend, and promised that the gala night would 'blazon the name of Hastings sky-wide'.

In a radio broadcast on Sunday 3rd September, the news which everyone had long dreaded was finally confirmed: Britain was at war with Germany. That afternoon Jack told his deputy Bill Greenhalf that he could go off duty at 5pm. At 9.30pm he asked Reeves, the night watchman, for the key to the office. During his shift Reeves did not see Jack again, which was not surprising as the piermaster went off duty at 10pm. Bill Greenhalf returned to work at 7am. Entering the seaward pavilion he saw a figure in the west wing of the stage, hanging by a noose from a girder fifteen feet above the ground. It looked like a dummy, hanged by someone as a tasteless joke. Perhaps it had a drawing of Hitler's face stuck on the front of its head. But as he got closer he could not believe his eyes: it was his boss, Jack, and he was dead.

Police surgeon Gordon Nesbitt Wood and Police Sergeant Bill Latchem arrived. Latchem cut down the body and the doctor, who by coincidence was Jack's GP, was able to assess the time of death, which he put at about midnight. They examined the scene. It was clear that Jack had used a nearby bench to

Alan Green and his boys in the 1930s.

Newspaper notice of events in 1939.

HASTINGS PIER

General Manager and Secretary: W. F. Brown   Piermaster: E. A. Mumford

ALAN RUSSELL presents the

REVELLERS

in " LAUGHTER UNLIMITED "
RADIO'S 1939 NEW STARS
NIGHTLY at 8 p.m.
SEATS: Reserved, 2/- and 1/6; Unreserved, 1/- and 6d. (inc. tax and toll).
MATINEES WEDNESDAY & SATURDAY at 3 p.m.   SEATS 4d., Toll 2d.

SPECIAL CONCERT EVERY SUNDAY at 8 p.m. by

THE REVELLERS AND ALAN GREEN'S BAND

BOX OFFICE OPEN ALL DAY   PHONE 60

HAPPY

HOLIDAY DANCES

WEDNESDAY, 8 p.m. to 1 a.m.   SATURDAY, 8 to 11.45 p.m.   Admission 1 6
MONDAY, TUESDAY, THURSDAY & FRIDAY, 7.30 to 10.30.   Admission 1 -

ALAN GREEN AND HIS BAND

Band Performances Daily at 11 a.m. and 3 p.m. (Wednesday and Saturday
11 a.m. only)   SEATS 2d.

EVERY WEEKDAY at 3.15 p.m.

PAULA BAIRD'S

CHILDREN'S HOUR

Magic, Mirth and Melody   ADULTS 6d., CHILDREN 3d.

reach the girder, tied one end of the rope around it and created a noose at the other end, placed his head through the loop then jumped off the bench. After being discreetly removed from the pier, Jack's body was conveyed to the RESH for the post mortem.

Coroner Harry Davenport Jones held an inquest that evening. Dr Nesbitt Wood gave the cause of death as syncope, due to dislocation of the neck by hanging. He was perplexed. Jack's rare visits to his surgery had been for trivial ailments; he had never suffered from nervous trouble or depression, but was 'a hearty individual' who was 'always cheerful'. Bill Greenhalf had worked with Jack for a year. When he last saw him, a few hours before his suicide, he was his usual self. Thomas Reeves agreed: Jack was 'always of a happy disposition' and Sunday night was no exception.

Jack left no suicide note, had made no plans or arrangements for his death, had no known entanglements, worries or problems. He had no debts; on the contrary, he lived well within his means and had saved up £149 (worth about £10,000 today), which he left to his mother. The coroner made vague suggestions: maybe he was worried about the war, or conscription, or the closure of the pier; or perhaps his mind became 'unbalanced'. The jury returned a verdict of suicide, because it could not have been anything else.

The funeral was held at the Borough Cemetery on 7th September. Over a hundred people attended, including twenty from Abbey Lodge, who dropped sprigs of acacia into his grave. A guard of honour was formed by Freemasons and pier workers. A director of the pier company, Captain A.M. Elliott,[1] paid glowing tribute to Jack, their 'most admirable Piermaster' and, unusually, made reference to the bewilderment everyone felt about his manner of death:

> I must express the deep and sincere regret of the board of directors and the officials at this terrible tragedy. Mr. Mumford had been in our employ over 15 years and always gave complete satisfaction. We liked and respected him and we cannot understand what can have induced him to do this rash thing. It is a terrible loss of a first class employee and, to some of us, a good friend.

The pier remained open to the public for eight months after war was declared. The Revellers finished their run and were followed by a comedy theatre troupe which had audiences rolling in the aisles. At forty-five Alan Green was too old to be conscripted, so his band was able to continue its residency until May 1940, when all performances on the pier were suspended. They played at other venues for the duration of the war. Alan tried to revive the idea of a 'Hastings Night' in London but, without Jack's enthusiasm and energy, the scheme had somehow lost its appeal and he quietly dropped it.

1. The solicitor who had acted for Joseph James in the chapter 'One Revolver; Two Dead'.

Was it mere coincidence that Jack took his life just hours after war was declared? As a boy he lived in Hastings throughout the previous conflict, and the town was barely affected. It was suggested that he may have feared conscription, but Jack was no coward. Besides, he was thirty-five and would not be called up for a long while, if at all: the war may have ended before his turn came. If the pier closed during the war then Jack would have been redeployed then reinstated when it was over.

Jack must have had a secret. Honour and reputation were paramount to men in his position and, if he feared that something was about to be exposed which had the power to destroy his good name, suicide may have felt like his only option. However, after his death no scandal was publicly revealed that might explain the tragic loss of one of the most popular men in Hastings. The case remains as perplexing today as it was back in 1939.

References: HSLO 10th September 1932; 26th August 1939; 2nd & 9th September 1939. *Hastings At War 1939-1945* by Nathan Dylan Goodwin, Phillimore, 2010.

Hastings Pier in the 1930s.

1948

CLIFF EDGE CONUNDRUM

ECCLESBOURNE

On 26th June 1943 a newly-wedded couple emerged from Holy Trinity church into both brilliant sunshine and married life. Doris, the beautiful teenage bride, wore a full-length dress of ivory satin and was flanked by two bridesmaids in pink taffeta. The immaculately turned-out groom, Syd, was a local celebrity, so nobody cared that he was twice her age; besides, the war had dragged on for nearly four years and people were entitled to grab happiness wherever they could find it.

Doris was the daughter of Captain J. Jacques RAMC. She grew up at 14 Saxon Mansions, St Leonards, until she was six, when her father walked out and never returned. In those days marital breakups were seen as shameful, so to avoid gossip her mother pretended to be a widow. In 1939 mother and daughter were living in rented rooms at 4 Braybrooke Terrace and Doris, fourteen, had left St Mary-in-the-Castle School and was working as an unqualified primary school assistant. During the war they moved to Flat 4, Abbotsford House, 4 Breeds Place, a Regency building on the seafront sandwiched between Mastin's department store and Pelham Crescent.

When Doris was eighteen her engagement was announced in the local paper: she was to marry a sergeant in the Royal Artillery, but that fell through and soon afterwards she was betrothed to Sydney Albert Gallop.

Syd was born in Hastings in 1907, the son of a master builder and a former housemaid. His father died when he was seven, and for the next thirty years he lived with his mother at 36 Priory Street, a terraced cottage long since demolished. He was a Civil Servant at Ore Place, a mansion off The Ridge. Though a 'steady and reliable worker', his passion lay not in curating army service records but in entertainment.

As a teenager Syd loved to clown around, and when he was twenty a local reporter dubbed him the 'funmaker-in-chief', and observed that his antics caused 'riotous laughter'. By the time he reached his thirties, Syd was the 'Mr Entertainment' of Hastings: nearly all of his free time was spent organising dances (with live orchestras), fancy dress balls and similar revelries. His likeability and quick wit made him the ideal compère. He co-founded, and was organising secretary of, the Merry Imps Vaudeville Entertainers,[1] for which he wrote songs, gags, parodies and farcical sketches; he also produced

1. 'Merry Imps' was the Junior Imperialist League, later called the Young Conservatives.

Breeds Place. The site is now covered by Muriel Matters House.

Ecclesbourne Glen.

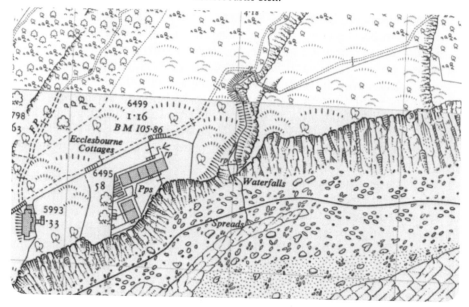

and directed its shows and performed in them as a singer and comedian. As secretary of the Revellers' Section of the Hastings Carnival Association he helped organise and direct Carnival Week, its Tiny Tots' Parade, Bathing Belles, Carnival Queen and comical burlesque circus.

Syd was not only a well-loved entertainer; he was a charming and highly literate man with impeccable manners and superb diplomatic skills. People who knew him said he was 'one of the most impartial men one could know' and an 'even-tempered chap who even in politics never got ruffled'. He was elected chairman of the Civil Service Clerical Association and of the local Conservative Association, where he was celebrated for his side-splitting impression of the sitting MP, Maurice Hely-Hutchinson.

When the Second World War was declared it was, of course, Syd who had the brilliant idea of forming a 'Blackout Social Club', offering a range of entertainments to cheer people's spirits, including party games, competitions and comedy turns. It was said that: 'During those difficult days he by his energy and enterprise steadfastly maintained an objective of the "get together and enjoy yourselves" spirit'.

Syd's hectic life left little time for romance and at thirty-six he was still living at home with his mum. Then he met Doris, an attractive teenager whose wedding had, rather embarrassingly, been publicly announced and subsequently cancelled. After a brief courtship he married her. They honeymooned in Llandudno then moved into a flat next door to Doris's mother: 10 Hanover House Royal, 6 Breeds Place.[1] Within two months the young bride was expecting a baby boy. His birth in May 1944 prompted a move to a house, 107 Stonefield Road.

Doris gave up work to raise their son, but Syd's life continued much as before. As well as working full time, and attending club and committee meetings, in just one year he organised a charity dance, a Guy Fawkes Carnival and Cabaret night, a Christmas Carnival, a St Patrick's Day Dance, a Topsy-Turvy Dance and a 'Salute the Soldier' Dance. Tickets for these events, held at the White Rock Pavilion, sold out quickly and, as compère, Syd would 'keep the evening's fun going non-stop', announcing novelty, exhibition and elimination dances, awarding spot prizes, telling wisecracks and generally jollying everyone along.

Syd's dedication to fun and frolics was noticed, valued and praised, as was his political work. When in February 1948 he resigned as chairman of the Young Conservatives, the party placed on record its deep appreciation of his twenty-five years of 'efficient and generous' service. The following month Syd compèred the Grand Conservative Ball at the Queen's Hotel for the final time.

The space vacated in his diary was swiftly filled by an even greater responsibility: in May he was elected organising secretary of the Hastings & St Leonards Charities' Association. Nobody could have predicted that, before he could attend his first meeting, Syd would be dead.

1. Hanover House was named for Prince George (grandson of George III) who stayed there in 1833.

At the time of his death, the Gallops' marriage was on the rocks, but Syd's account of it died with him, leaving only Doris's, which she related at his inquest. According to her, every minute of his free time was devoted to organising entertainments, depriving her of the attention a wife deserved. Worse, he was like Dr Jekyll and Mr Hyde. Behind closed doors the amiable optimist became 'moody, difficult and bad-tempered'. Their marriage was over within weeks, but she did not leave because she was already pregnant. Since then she had steadfastly refused sexual relations. They argued about that, and about her dating other men, yet Syd stubbornly refused to grant her a divorce.

Doris claimed that Syd had slashed his wrists and tried to gas himself, and had also made an attempt to kill her. On the morning of the day he died, 2nd June 1948, he had opened the gas tap in her bedroom, hoping to asphyxiate her as she slept. That same evening she voluntarily went with her — suicidal and homicidal — husband for a walk along an unfenced clifftop, and stopped for a chat near the edge, with nothing between them and a sheer 300ft drop.

Their son, who had just turned four, was left at home alone as they set out at 7.30pm to walk the one-and-a-half miles to Ecclesbourne Glen. From the crown of the East Hill they strolled across the headland, over the wooden bridge and up the steeply rising path until they were about 300ft above sea level. It was approaching 9pm and getting dark when Syd turned down a narrow path to the cliff edge and peered over, saying that his life was 'not worth living'. Doris told him to think of his work, his home, his son and his dear old mother, who was dependent on him.

They walked along a gully running parallel with the cliff edge, known locally (she said) as 'Lovers' Leap', and stood looking out to sea. Suddenly, she felt the earth beneath her feet give way, but quickly regained her footing. Syd remarked that anyone who went over the cliff 'would not stand much chance'. As he pointed to some gulls floating in the sea below, she leaned forward to peer over the edge at them and, as she straightened up,

My left leg seemed to give in front of me and my other leg seemed to collapse. I fell onto the ground. I closed my eyes and expected to fall. I did not fall very far. I felt a jerk as if something has stopped me and later found that the handle of my umbrella had broken. At the same moment I rolled over and grabbed at something solid with my right hand. I pulled myself up into a kneeling position, threw my head back and looked. I saw nothing. My husband had gone.

'At the time I thought he had tried to murder me by pushing me over the cliff', she explained. Obeying her gut instinct she ran away from the scene then walked briskly to her mother's flat. Arriving at about 9.30pm she told Mrs Jacques and her 'fancy man' Harry that she feared Syd might harm their son. They walked with her to Stonefield Road but Syd was not there and the boy was fine. They went to the police station and reported everything that had happened.

At daybreak on 3rd June a police search party led by Detective Inspector Stanley Copper[1] found Syd's corpse on the pebble beach at the foot of the cliffs, 300 yards east of the glen. His wristwatch had stopped at 9.14. Overnight the tide had come in, covered him, and then ebbed away. After photographing the scene police recovered the body by boat. Doris's brother gave formal identification and the police surgeon, Dr G. Nesbitt Wood, carried out a post mortem.

That evening DS Longhurst collected Doris in a police car and drove her to the place she last saw Syd, so she could describe precisely what happened. He found no sign of a struggle. Seven or eight feet down the cliff face was a slither mark and what appeared to be a heel mark. There was also an imprint of a woman's shoe three feet over the edge of the cliff, on a grass ledge and just inches from where the cliff face fell off sheer. Everything supported Doris's story. There were no witnesses to the scene at the cliff edge, but she had seen four girls and two men on the cliffs that night. The police traced the men, Edward Stonham and John Woolner. One remembered a couple quarrelling 'like any man and wife'; the other passed them at 8pm then saw Doris on her own at 9.15pm, 'hurrying' and 'very flushed'. The girls, Polish and Czech pupils at the Queen's School at Fairlight Hall, had seen nothing of interest.

Syd's funeral was held at the Borough Cemetery on 7th June. The vicar of Emmanuel church officiated and mourners included representatives of clubs and charities, shocked that such a lovely man had met such a violent end, and sad for his fatherless baby. Two letters of condolence were published in the *HSLO*; one extended sympathy to his mother; the other mentioned his mother's great loss. Neither mentioned his widow. After Syd was buried Doris reverted to her maiden name, an extraordinary and disrespectful act for a newly-bereaved widow with a young child, whom she deprived of his father's surname.

Doris gave an interview to the *Daily Mirror*: 'A lot of people in Hastings have made up their minds about how my husband died', she said. 'My conscience is quite clear. Sydney and I had something serious to discuss and we went for a walk on the cliffs. Something happened there — it was not a quarrel — but a few seconds afterwards I found myself on my hands and knees and Sydney was gone. I did not know whether he had gone away or had gone over the cliff.'

Having initially told the police that she was happily married, Doris later contradicted herself. The reason for the discrepancy, she said, was the couple's attempt to 'keep it as quiet as we could. We did not want anyone to know our troubles'. Harry Wadlow stated that Syd did not mind Doris attending dances with people her own age. However, Edward Gibson recalled that Syd minded very much, and had tackled her more than once about dating other men. She had told him not to worry, as 'it would all be settled by 4th June'. When pressed to explain, she said 'Ronnie' was going away on that date.

---

1. Copper's claim to fame, apart from his comically appropriate surname, was that, in 1937, he was the first policeman in Sussex to be trained at Hendon Police College.

The bridge and steep path followed by Mr and Mrs Gallop.

On 12th June an inquest was held in the oak-panelled courtroom in Hastings Town Hall. The story was so sensational that it was covered by five national daily newspapers as well as the regional press across Britain. Described as a 'tall, attractive brunette', Doris was suitably attired in a jet black costume, topped with an off-the-face straw hat and a half-veil. She was the first and only significant witness, her testimony took two hours and, when questioned, she answered without faltering.

The coroner was acutely aware of local gossip and told the jury to ignore it. Whilst it was true that 'possible verdicts included murder', that would require proof that Doris had 'deliberately and with malice aforethought pushed him over', and he saw no evidence of that. It could have been suicide, a failed attempt (by Syd) at murder-and-suicide, or an accident in which Doris stumbled and her husband lost his footing trying to save her life. He alluded twice to the suggestion that Doris had pushed Syd, and advised her that, if she feared a question might incriminate her, she was 'entitled to refuse to answer it'.

As Doris concluded her evidence there was 'a stir from the back of the court'. Annie, Syd's seventy-nine-year-old mother, 'stood up dramatically' and announced firmly, in her Glaswegian accent: 'I want to speak against this!' She was helped to a seat at the witness table and, fixing her daughter-in-law with a hard and accusatory stare, declared angrily: 'My son loved you right through'. The coroner invited Annie to ask questions, and there followed 'a tense moment' as Doris sat with 'a drawn face and clenched hands', whilst Annie told her: 'Your tale is a pack of lies! My son may have had faults, but one of them was that he loved his wife too much'. The coroner intervened: 'I'm not going to have a scene in this court'. Annie turned to him and, in a tone of disgust, replied: 'Even her own mother told my son he should give her a good hiding'.

In the weeks before Syd's death, Doris had been seeing two other men. When questioned about them she prevaricated and contradicted herself. First she stated that Syd was jealous and 'objected to any friends I might make'; then she claimed that he 'made no objection' to her going to dances with men. The atmosphere in court was electric when a man she had been going about with took the stand to be questioned.

Doris sat with her head bowed as the aforementioned 'Ronnie' gave his deposition. A tall, handsome ex-soldier with smoothly-brushed fair hair, he had been demobbed in January and met Doris at Easter. She called herself 'Deirdre' and told him that her marriage had been annulled and she was housekeeper to Syd Gallop. When Ronnie called for her he met Syd, who raised no objection to him taking her out. Syd's mother was invited to question Ronnie. In a tone of sheer contempt she asked if he were not 'ashamed to be going out with a married woman'. Clearly appalled by his conduct, she continued: 'You went to her home at 10 o'clock at night. My son said to her: "Get him out of here"'. The coroner felt he needed to remind the jury that: 'However much you may disapprove of the way this couple were carrying on their married life, this is not a court of morals'. The all-male jury took just five minutes to return an open verdict.

Open verdict on man over cliff: 'He tried to push me'—widow

Mr. Gallop.

FAIR-HAIRED Mrs. Doris Mary Gallop, 23, widow of Sidney Gallop, who fell to his death over a cliff at Hastings, Sussex, and a man friend were "cross-examined" by her mother-in-law during a five-hour inquest—at which an open verdict was returned—yesterday.

Mrs. Gallop said she and her husband had been arguing about divorce on the cliff top. She thought he tried to murder her by pushing her over the cliff.

Ronald Dean, of St. Mary-road, Hastings, said he and Mrs. Gallop had been friendly since Easter, but he did not know she was married.

She told him her marriage had been annulled and she was Gallop's housekeeper, he added.

"Are You Not Ashamed?"

Gallop's mother asked him if he was not ashamed at going out with a married woman.

Mrs. Doris Gallop
"It flashed through my mind he had tried to kill me . . my impulse was to run."

CLIFF-FALL WIDOW WEDS
Four months after inquest on husband

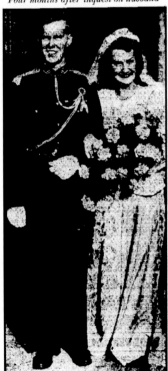

CLIFF WIDOW IS ACCUSED: 'ALL LIES'

By mother-in-law

From ANTHONY HUNTER,
Daily Mail Reporter

HASTINGS, Friday.

AFTER two hours of intensive questioning by the Hastings coroner and a police solicitor attractive 23-year-old Mrs. Doris Mary Gallop faced her frail 71-year-old mother-in-law across the witness table here today.

With drawn face and clenched hands she heard Mrs. Annis Gallop whisper: "Your tale is a pack of lies."

Doris and Ronnie left the courtroom separately. When tackled by eager pressmen waiting outside, Ronnie told them: 'I do not know whether I am prepared to carry on this friendship with Mrs Gallop. I shall meet her again but I want time to think things over'. He did not need much time: sixteen weeks after Syd's death, Ronnie married Doris at Emmanuel church in Priory Road. The wedding was not covered by the *HSLO*, but prompted by Doris's notoriety the *Daily Mail* ran a story, complete with a photograph. The bride did not wear a wedding gown but a floor-length skirt and matching jacket in a pale colour, whilst the groom wore the dress uniform of his regiment, the King's Troop, Royal Artillery, complete with gleaming shoulder chains and looped braid cap-lines.

In line with tradition, Doris and her son took Ronnie's surname, but she also changed her forename. The couple had one child together. They spent the rest of their lives in Hastings, where Ronnie followed a career as a college lecturer. The marriage was a long and happy one, and they celebrated their diamond wedding anniversary in 2008. She died in 2015; he outlived her by three years, expiring at the age of ninety-seven.

References: *HSLO* 11th June 1927, 12th June & 19th June 1948; Joe Aldridge in the *HSLO* 19th June 1948 and Kay Hayes in the *HSLO* 7th August 1948. Press cuttings opposite: (top) *Daily Mirror* 4th June 1948; *Daily Mail* 12th June & (wedding) 18th October 1948.

Ecclesbourne Cliffs.

STRANGE EXITS VOLUME II

More bizarre deaths in Hastings between 1740 and 1958

NOTABLE SUSSEX WOMEN

Winner of the *Writers' News* Local History Prize, this beautifully produced
hardback contains biographical sketches of 580 notable individuals.
Its 304 pages include 32 pages of gloss photographic plates.

WOMEN OF VICTORIAN SUSSEX

Examines the lives of women living in Sussex around the middle
of the 19th century, exploring their status, their employment
and their dealings with the law. By letting the facts speak for
themselves, the book builds up a devastating critique of a profoundly
unjust and hypocritical society. Illustrated paperback.

For author-signed copies, order from www.hastingspress.co.uk
or Paypal to hastings.press@gmail.com
Each book is £10. Postage is £2.50 for one and £3 for two books.